Jammin'
JUMBLE®

Puzzle Fun for Everyone

Henri Arnold, Bob Lee,
and Mike Argirion

TRIUMPH
B O O K S
CHICAGO

This book is available in quantity at special discounts
for your group or organization.

For further information, contact:

Triumph Books
542 South Dearborn Street
Suite 750
Chicago, Illinois 60605
(312) 939-3330
Fax (312) 663-3557

Printed in U.S.A.

ISBN-13: 978-1-57243-844-6
ISBN-10: 1-57243-844-4

Design by Sue Knopf

CONTENTS

Jammin' JUMBLE®

Classic Puzzles

JUMBLE®

Unscramble these four Jumbles, one letter to each square, to form four ordinary words.

NITHK

ENCEF

MILTEG

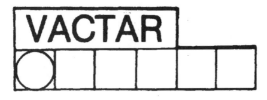

VACTAR

DON'T EXPECT SOME-
ONE TO TALK
TURKEY WHO'S THIS.

Now arrange the circled letters to form the surprise answer, as suggested by the above cartoon.

Print answer here

JUMBLE®

Unscramble these four Jumbles, one letter to each square, to form four ordinary words.

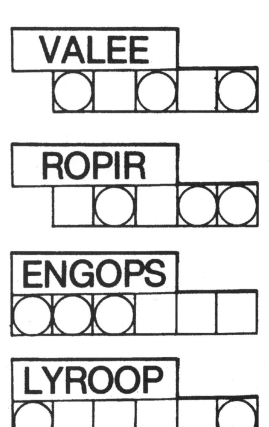

VALEE

ROPIR

ENGOPS

LYROOP

IF YOU THINK GOLF IS ONLY A RICH MAN'S GAME, LOOK AT THESE.

Now arrange the circled letters to form the surprise answer, as suggested by the above cartoon.

Print answer here   ALL THE ☐☐☐☐ ☐☐☐☐☐☐

JUMBLE®

Unscramble these four Jumbles, one letter to each square, to form four ordinary words.

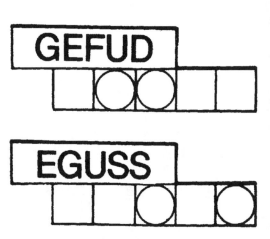

GEFUD

EGUSS

WHARTT

GLOIBE

WHAT SOME WORK IN THE GARDEN CAN LEAVE ONE.

Now arrange the circled letters to form the surprise answer, as suggested by the above cartoon.

Print answer here " "

JUMBLE®

Unscramble these four Jumbles, one letter to each square, to form four ordinary words.

TYREN

DRAIP

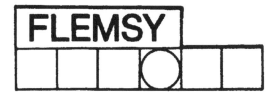

FLEMSY

SHARTH

WHAT THE GUY WHO IGNORED HIS WIFE WHEN SHE SUGGESTED THAT THEY BUY A SECOND CAR TURNED OUT TO BE.

Now arrange the circled letters to form the surprise answer, as suggested by the above cartoon.

Print answer here A

JUMBLE®

Unscramble these four Jumbles, one letter to
each square, to form four ordinary words.

DOLOB

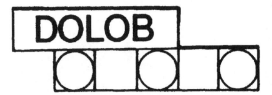
NOUGY

REWAYL

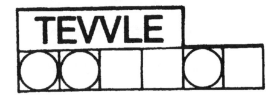
TEVVLE

What do you suggest?

WHAT HIS CURLY
HAIR WAS BEGINNING
TO DO.

Now arrange the circled letters to form the
surprise answer, as suggested by the above
cartoon.

Print answer here ☐☐☐☐ ☐☐☐☐☐ – ☐☐☐

JUMBLE®

Unscramble these four Jumbles, one letter to each square, to form four ordinary words.

GLIVI

WYLEN

PANTIC

ABAANN

Nobody's keeping me from hitting the bull's eye

WHAT THE ARCHER WAS.

Now arrange the circled letters to form the surprise answer, as suggested by the above cartoon.

Print answer here "⬡⬡⬡⬡" ON ⬡⬡⬡⬡⬡⬡⬡⬡

JUMBLE®

Unscramble these four Jumbles, one letter to
each square, to form four ordinary words.

TRYAR

ALTEM

NUCHAH

FROMIN

WHAT A REAL
FIRM MAKES THAT
MAY GO OFF IN
THE HEAT.

Now arrange the circled letters to form the
surprise answer, as suggested by the above
cartoon.

Print answer here A " ☐☐☐☐☐ ☐☐☐☐☐☐ "

JUMBLE®

Unscramble these four Jumbles, one letter to each square, to form four ordinary words.

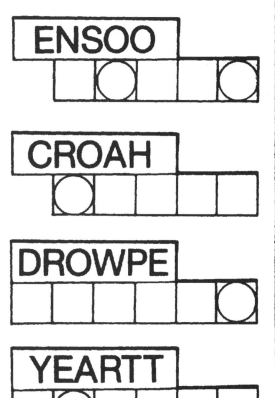

ENSOO

CROAH

DROWPE

YEARTT

Now arrange the circled letters to form the surprise answer, as suggested by the above cartoon.

Print answer here " ⬡⬡⬡⬡⬡ "

JUMBLE®

Unscramble these four Jumbles, one letter to each square, to form four ordinary words.

OMBOL

YAHND

STUJAD

UPTIME

What kind of vegetables do you have?

IT'S A CASE OF PEAS OR BEANS.

Now arrange the circled letters to form the surprise answer, as suggested by the above cartoon.

Print answer here

JUMBLE®

Unscramble these four Jumbles, one letter to each square, to form four ordinary words.

BUJOM

ACOOC

NORMAT

DARZIL

Roll up your sleeve. We have to take some tests

ANOTHER NAME FOR DRACULA.

Now arrange the circled letters to form the surprise answer, as suggested by the above cartoon.

Print answer here THE ⬭⬭⬭⬭⬭⬭ ⬭⬭⬭⬭⬭

JUMBLE®

Unscramble these four Jumbles, one letter to
each square, to form four ordinary words.

HOACC

PREKO

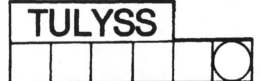
TULYSS

YEEHRB

Speech: It's plagiarism! It's not!

WHAT YOU MIGHT
HAVE WHEN TWO
AUTHORS SUE
EACH OTHER.

Now arrange the circled letters to form the
surprise answer, as suggested by the above
cartoon.

Print answer here **A**

12

JUMBLE®

Unscramble these four Jumbles, one letter to each square, to form four ordinary words.

YODIL

DIGUE

GLEMIN

TISSAD

WHAT THE ABSENT-MINDED HEN DID.

Now arrange the circled letters to form the surprise answer, as suggested by the above cartoon.

Print answer here

AN

JUMBLE®

Unscramble these four Jumbles, one letter to each square, to form four ordinary words.

TALEV

GAGBY

YOMARR

VOCENX

HOW THEY ACTED AT THE UNDERTAKERS' ANNUAL SHINDIG.

Now arrange the circled letters to form the surprise answer, as suggested by the above cartoon.

Print answer here

JUMBLE

Unscramble these four Jumbles, one letter to each square, to form four ordinary words.

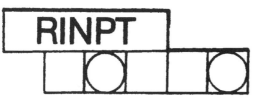

RINPT

ZUFYZ

UTTOLE

MEDOCY

COULD IT BE
A SOUND FROM
A DOG WITHOUT
A PEDIGREE?

Now arrange the circled letters to form the surprise answer, as suggested by the above cartoon.

Print answer here A " ⬡⬡⬡⬡ – ⬡⬡ "

JUMBLE®

Unscramble these four Jumbles, one letter to each square, to form four ordinary words.

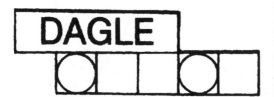

DAGLE

PRYAT

CAGNEY

LIMBEN

WHAT A DENTIST MIGHT DO ABOUT THOSE MISSING TEETH.

Now arrange the circled letters to form the surprise answer, as suggested by the above cartoon.

Print answer here "◯◯◯◯◯◯" THE ◯◯◯

JUMBLE®

Unscramble these four Jumbles, one letter to
each square, to form four ordinary words.

KREAM

VALAN

PLATEA

DRAUWP

COULD IT HAVE
BEEN A DRAMA
ABOUT A FAMOUS
FLEET?

Now arrange the circled letters to form the
surprise answer, as suggested by the above
cartoon.

Print answer here

JUMBLE®

Unscramble these four Jumbles, one letter to each square, to form four ordinary words.

ZIMEA

POAYS

SUNDOL

CUPSAM

MUSIC THAT MIGHT ACCOMPANY A TURKEY DINNER.

Now arrange the circled letters to form the surprise answer, as suggested by the above cartoon.

Print answer here   A "◯◯◯" ◯◯◯◯◯◯◯◯

JUMBLE®

Unscramble these four Jumbles, one letter to
each square, to form four ordinary words.

PERIT

ELVOH

GOSTEO

FOUTTI

WHAT THE GUY WHO
STOLE A BANANA
GAVE THE COPS.

Now arrange the circled letters to form the
surprise answer, as suggested by the above
cartoon.

Print answer here ⬚⬚⬚ ⬚⬚⬚⬚

JUMBLE®

Unscramble these four Jumbles, one letter to each square, to form four ordinary words.

CUROC

HIKKA

KORBEN

SOOPUR

HOW DOES THAT FISHERMAN WHO TENDS SHEEP ON THE SIDE MAKE A LIVING?

Now arrange the circled letters to form the surprise answer, as suggested by the above cartoon.

Print answer here BY  OR BY

JUMBLE®

Unscramble these four Jumbles, one letter to
each square, to form four ordinary words.

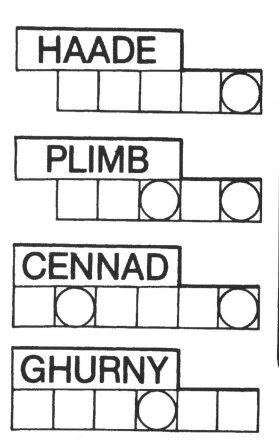

HAADE

PLIMB

CENNAD

GHURNY

IF JOY IS THE
OPPOSITE OF
SORROW, WHAT'S THE
OPPOSITE OF WOE?

Now arrange the circled letters to form the
surprise answer, as suggested by the above
cartoon.

Print answer here

JUMBLE®

Unscramble these four Jumbles, one letter to each square, to form four ordinary words.

LELOH

CAIBS

YARFFA

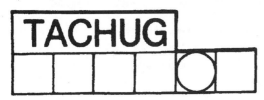

TACHUG

Ain't he something?

WHAT KIND OF A GUY WAS THAT PRESS PHOTOGRAPHER?

Now arrange the circled letters to form the surprise answer, as suggested by the above cartoon.

Print answer here A ⬭⬭⬭⬭⬭⬭ ONE

JUMBLE®

Unscramble these four Jumbles, one letter to
each square, to form four ordinary words.

NOICT

POSOT

INSOOP

SOUNIC

EVERYTHING YOU
SHOULD KNOW ABOUT
ENTRANCES AND
EXITS.

Now arrange the circled letters to form the
surprise answer, as suggested by the above
cartoon.

Print answer here THE ◯◯◯ & ◯◯◯◯

JUMBLE®

Unscramble these four Jumbles, one letter to each square, to form four ordinary words.

GINOR

BREHT

DOHOKE

SENTOL

WHAT HE WAS, AFTER HE BOUGHT HER THAT BIG DIAMOND.

Now arrange the circled letters to form the surprise answer, as suggested by the above cartoon.

Print answer here

JUMBLE®

Unscramble these four Jumbles, one letter to each square, to form four ordinary words.

VEROL

MALFE

TIPOLE

YISMAL

COUNSELOR

Next!

HE WORKS OUT
THE PROBLEMS OF
"MIXED-UP" LOVERS.

Now arrange the circled letters to form the surprise answer, as suggested by the above cartoon.

Print answer here " ◯◯◯◯◯◯ "

JUMBLE®

Unscramble these four Jumbles, one letter to each square, to form four ordinary words.

RILLT

NUBOD

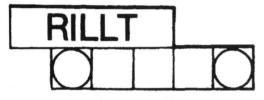

VOGNER

BERBOR

CLANG! CLANG!

WHAT THE LOCKSMITH MADE WHEN HIS SHOP CAUGHT FIRE.

Now arrange the circled letters to form the surprise answer, as suggested by the above cartoon.

Print answer here

 A ☐☐☐☐ FOR THE  ☐☐☐☐

Daily Puzzles

JUMBLE®

Unscramble these four Jumbles, one letter to each square, to form four ordinary words.

CHULG

HIDUM

REZIFE

LESING

She sounds better than ever

THE SOPRANO STOOD ON THE BALCONY SO SHE COULD DO THIS.

Now arrange the circled letters to form the surprise answer, as suggested by the above cartoon.

Print answer here "   "

JUMBLE®

Unscramble these four Jumbles, one letter to each square, to form four ordinary words.

TYFFI

PROUG

GININN

RIVFEY

Such a sponger--
never even
remembers to
say thank you

And never
reciprocates

HE'S ALWAYS
FORGETTING, BUT
NEVER THIS.

Now arrange the circled letters to form the surprise answer, as suggested by the above cartoon.

Print answer here "◯◯◯ ◯◯◯◯◯◯"

JUMBLE®

Unscramble these four Jumbles, one letter to each square, to form four ordinary words.

SILAA

MEERB

CELLOA

KLUSCE

GENERAL STORE

HOW MUCH DID A BELT USED TO COST?

Now arrange the circled letters to form the surprise answer, as suggested by the above cartoon.

Print answer here

 THAN "  — "

JUMBLE®

Unscramble these four Jumbles, one letter to
each square, to form four ordinary words.

LEZBA

ALCKO

NAULCY

CAPTEK

You'll live through it

SALON

WHAT IT TAKES
TO HAVE NO
EYEBROWS.

Now arrange the circled letters to form the
surprise answer, as suggested by the above
cartoon.

Print answer here A ⬡⬡⬡ OF ⬡⬡⬡⬡⬡

JUMBLE®

Unscramble these four Jumbles, one letter to each square, to form four ordinary words.

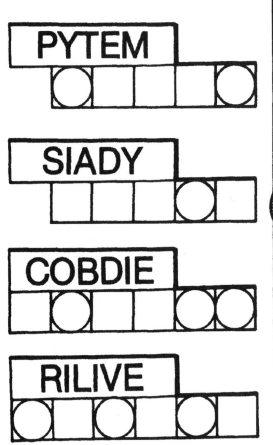

PYTEM

SIADY

COBDIE

RILIVE

THEIR RELATIVE WHO WAS KNOWN FOR HIS STINGINESS MUST HAVE BEEN THIS.

Now arrange the circled letters to form the surprise answer, as suggested by the above cartoon.

Print answer here

JUMBLE®

Unscramble these four Jumbles, one letter to each square, to form four ordinary words.

RETIG

AFTEC

TINBAD

CROSCH

IF YOU WANT TO RELAX AT DINNER, TAKE THIS BEFORE EACH MEAL.

Now arrange the circled letters to form the surprise answer, as suggested by the above cartoon.

Print answer here

JUMBLE®

Unscramble these four Jumbles, one letter to each square, to form four ordinary words.

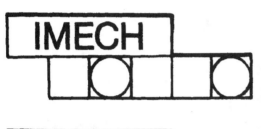

IMECH

NYSAP

CLEFEE

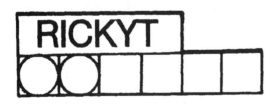

RICKYT

Hey, Mom--- LOOK!

MIGHT BE ENOUGH TO TURN YOUR HAIR WHITE SUDDENLY!

Now arrange the circled letters to form the surprise answer, as suggested by the above cartoon.

Print answer here

JUMBLE®

Unscramble these four Jumbles, one letter to each square, to form four ordinary words.

CHARN

EDDIC

NUTBOT

TYFARC

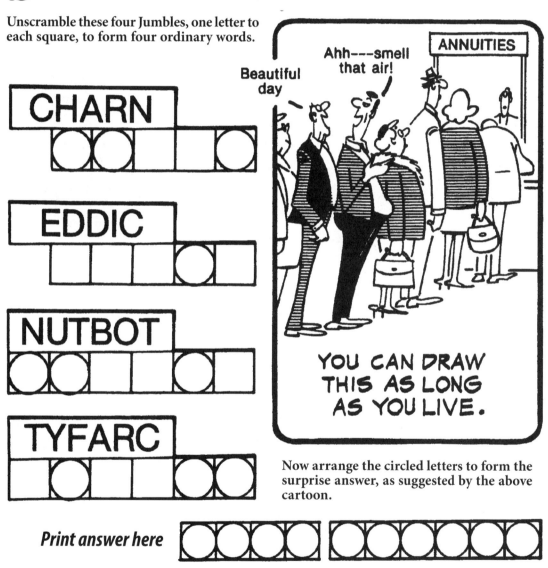

Now arrange the circled letters to form the surprise answer, as suggested by the above cartoon.

Print answer here

JUMBLE®

Unscramble these four Jumbles, one letter to
each square, to form four ordinary words.

HECAF

MASCK

FORTYS

LUFUES

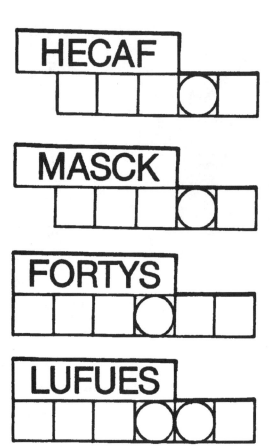

THEY SOMETIMES
HOLD HANDS AT THE
POLICE STATION.

Now arrange the circled letters to form the
surprise answer, as suggested by the above
cartoon.

Print answer here

JUMBLE®

Unscramble these four Jumbles, one letter to each square, to form four ordinary words.

INJOG

ARICH

TOMELE

CISTEB

Do you have any change?

PEOPLE LIKE TO HELP HIM OUT, AS SOON AS---

Now arrange the circled letters to form the surprise answer, as suggested by the above cartoon.

Print answer here

JUMBLE®

Unscramble these four Jumbles, one letter to each square, to form four ordinary words.

YOSUL

STAIV

FLUINS

LEEBIF

HE SAID HE WAS LIVING IN THE PRESENT---

Now arrange the circled letters to form the surprise answer, as suggested by the above cartoon.

Print answer here " ⬡⬡⬡⬡⬡ "

JUMBLE®

Unscramble these four Jumbles, one letter to each square, to form four ordinary words.

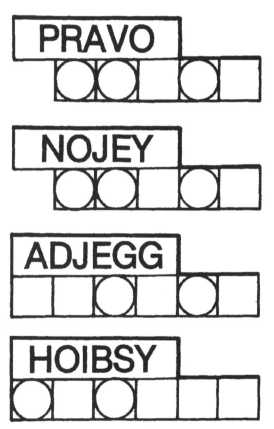

PRAVO

NOJEY

ADJEGG

HOIBSY

I'm off to gay Paree

WHAT TO SAY WHEN YOUR FRIENDLY SKELETON LEAVES ON VACATION.

Now arrange the circled letters to form the surprise answer, as suggested by the above cartoon.

Print answer here " ⬭⬭⬭⬭ ⬭⬭⬭⬭⬭ "

JUMBLE®

Unscramble these four Jumbles, one letter to each square, to form four ordinary words.

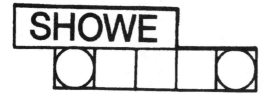

Now arrange the circled letters to form the surprise answer, as suggested by the above cartoon.

Print answer here

JUMBLE®

Unscramble these four Jumbles, one letter to each square, to form four ordinary words.

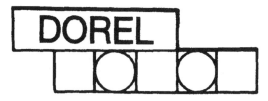

DOREL

NORIM

EDUCAD

LANFIE

WHAT'S THE BEST DISH TO GET AT A "GREASY SPOON" RESTAURANT?

Now arrange the circled letters to form the surprise answer, as suggested by the above cartoon.

Print answer here

JUMBLE®

Unscramble these four Jumbles, one letter to
each square, to form four ordinary words.

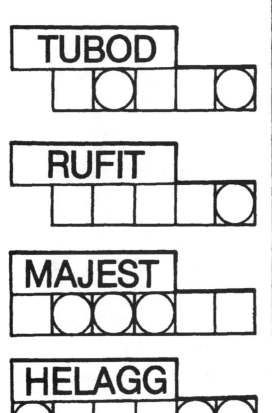

TUBOD

RUFIT

MAJEST

HELAGG

Those old
sayings get
tiresome

WHAT MANY
"OLD SAWS"
HAVE DONE.

Now arrange the circled letters to form the
surprise answer, as suggested by the above
cartoon.

*Print answer
here*

 THEIR

JUMBLE®

Unscramble these four Jumbles, one letter to each square, to form four ordinary words.

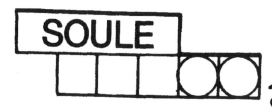

SOULE

HEWIG

TESSMY

GIANAU

SOME GUYS ARE WISE, AND SOME ARE THIS.

Now arrange the circled letters to form the surprise answer, as suggested by the above cartoon.

Print answer here

JUMBLE®

Unscramble these four Jumbles, one letter to each square, to form four ordinary words.

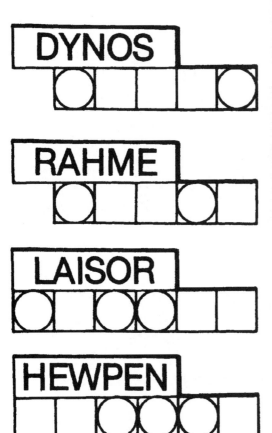

DYNOS

RAHME

LAISOR

HEWPEN

WHAT AN OLD-FASHIONED HUSBAND EXPECTS HIS WIFE TO DO.

Now arrange the circled letters to form the surprise answer, as suggested by the above cartoon.

Print answer here

 HIM WITH THE

JUMBLE®

Unscramble these four Jumbles, one letter to each square, to form four ordinary words.

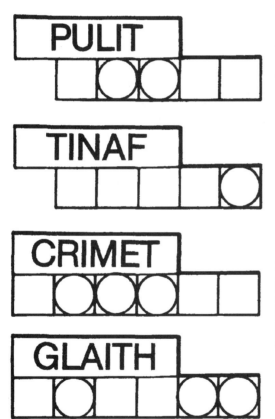

PULIT

TINAF

CRIMET

GLAITH

My dear--you look divine

But you could lose a few pounds

SOME PEOPLE ARE TACTFUL, WHILE OTHERS DO THIS.

Now arrange the circled letters to form the surprise answer, as suggested by the above cartoon.

Print answer here ⬡⬡⬡⬡ THE ⬡⬡⬡⬡⬡

JUMBLE®

Unscramble these four Jumbles, one letter to each square, to form four ordinary words.

NAGLD

YOGUN

TENTAX

ROCCEE

But they're getting golden parachutes

WHAT HAPPENED TO THOSE EXECUTIVES WHEN THERE WAS A TAKEOVER AT THE FOOD-PROCESSING COMPANY.

Now arrange the circled letters to form the surprise answer, as suggested by the above cartoon.

Print answer here THEY ☐☐☐ " ☐☐☐☐☐☐☐ "

JUMBLE®

Unscramble these four Jumbles, one letter to each square, to form four ordinary words.

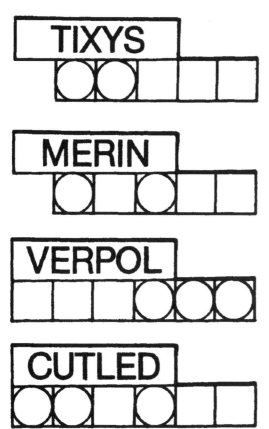

TIXYS

MERIN

VERPOL

CUTLED

A MAN USUALLY CAN'T THINK STRAIGHT WHEN HE ONLY HAS THIS.

Now arrange the circled letters to form the surprise answer, as suggested by the above cartoon.

Print answer here  ON HIS

JUMBLE

Unscramble these four Jumbles, one letter to each square, to form four ordinary words.

SYSUF

HAGUL

LUBBEA

MILTEG

HE WHO INDULGES----

Now arrange the circled letters to form the surprise answer, as suggested by the above cartoon.

Print answer here

JUMBLE®

Unscramble these four Jumbles, one letter to each square, to form four ordinary words.

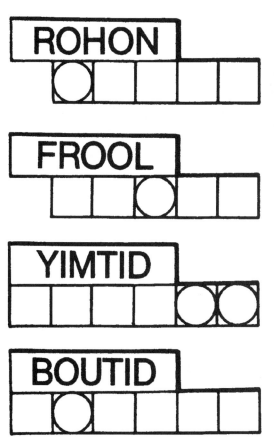

ROHON

FROOL

YIMTID

BOUTID

THIS MIGHT BE MORE APPRECIATED IF WE WERE GIVEN IT LATER IN LIFE.

Now arrange the circled letters to form the surprise answer, as suggested by the above cartoon.

Print answer here

JUMBLE®

Unscramble these four Jumbles, one letter to each square, to form four ordinary words.

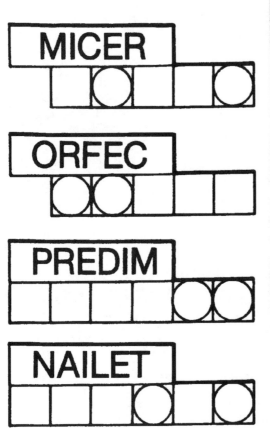

MICER

ORFEC

PREDIM

NAILET

Have another one on the house

HE'S SUPPOSED TO BE WORKING AT THE DOCK FOR PAY, BUT HE PREFERS TO DO THIS.

Now arrange the circled letters to form the surprise answer, as suggested by the above cartoon.

Print answer here

JUMBLE

Unscramble these four Jumbles, one letter to each square, to form four ordinary words.

DRYIT

REQUE

MELVUL

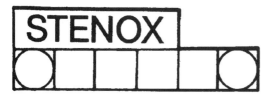

STENOX

WHY HIS CONSCIENCE
WAS CLEAN.

Now arrange the circled letters to form the surprise answer, as suggested by the above cartoon.

Print answer here HE ⬡⬡⬡⬡⬡ ⬡⬡⬡⬡ IT

JUMBLE®

Unscramble these four Jumbles, one letter to each square, to form four ordinary words.

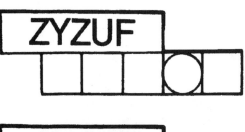

ZYZUF

NAUHM

LAVOAW

DOSPYR

This isn't easy

WHAT THAT BUFFET DINNER WAS SORT OF.

Now arrange the circled letters to form the surprise answer, as suggested by the above cartoon.

Print answer here " ◯◯◯ – ◯◯◯◯◯◯◯ "

JUMBLE®

Unscramble these four Jumbles, one letter to each square, to form four ordinary words.

THILG

WALOG

BOBING

ENNOIT

WHAT SOME
EVENING DRESSES
ARE.

Now arrange the circled letters to form the surprise answer, as suggested by the above cartoon.

Print answer here MORE ⬡⬡⬡⬡ THAN ⬡⬡⬡⬡

JUMBLE®

Unscramble these four Jumbles, one letter to
each square, to form four ordinary words.

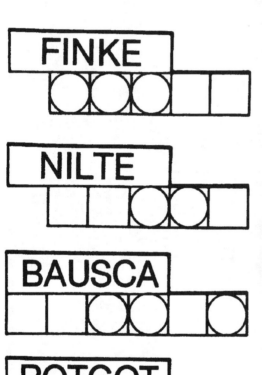

FINKE

NILTE

BAUSCA

ROTGOT

WHERE THE
FANATIC'S TRAIN
OF THOUGHT
ALWAYS RAN.

Now arrange the circled letters to form the
surprise answer, as suggested by the above
cartoon.

*Print answer
here* ON
A

JUMBLE®

Unscramble these four Jumbles, one letter to each square, to form four ordinary words.

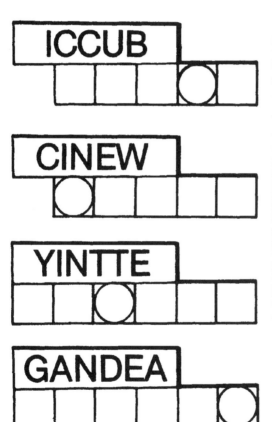

ICCUB

CINEW

YINTTE

GANDEA

There were some bargains I just couldn't resist

HER PROMISE TO BE ON TIME CARRIED A LOT OF THIS.

Now arrange the circled letters to form the surprise answer, as suggested by the above cartoon.

Print answer here

55

JUMBLE®

Unscramble these four Jumbles, one letter to each square, to form four ordinary words.

SEMYS

YOWDD

DIBITT

UNDASE

WHAT THE EPIDEMIC OF MEASLES IN GENEVA CREATED.

Now arrange the circled letters to form the surprise answer, as suggested by the above cartoon.

Print answer here

JUMBLE®

Unscramble these four Jumbles, one letter to
each square, to form four ordinary words.

ABNIS

WONNK

CRESPO

GANFIC

WHAT HE WAS AS
A RESULT OF
TEACHING HIS TEEN-
AGER TO DRIVE.

Now arrange the circled letters to form the
surprise answer, as suggested by the above
cartoon.

Print answer here

JUMBLE®

Unscramble these four Jumbles, one letter to each square, to form four ordinary words.

STYRT

GRITE

BARNEY

GLINTE

WHAT SHE SERVED THE HANDSOME DEPOSITOR WITH.

Now arrange the circled letters to form the surprise answer, as suggested by the above cartoon.

Print answer here

JUMBLE®

Unscramble these four Jumbles, one letter to each square, to form four ordinary words.

VALAN

OBOAT

COORTH

WANEDD

WHAT THE SNOWBALL FIGHT PROVED TO BE.

Now arrange the circled letters to form the surprise answer, as suggested by the above cartoon.

Print answer here A

JUMBLE®

Unscramble these four Jumbles, one letter to each square, to form four ordinary words.

ENSOO

ENCIE

TRARAT

VERROF

THE PART OF THE BOOK THE PODIATRIST LIKED BEST.

Now arrange the circled letters to form the surprise answer, as suggested by the above cartoon.

Print answer here THE

JUMBLE®

Unscramble these four Jumbles, one letter to each square, to form four ordinary words.

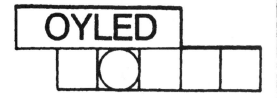

OYLED

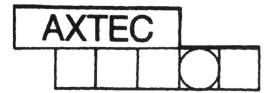

AXTEC

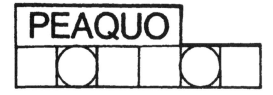

PEAQUO

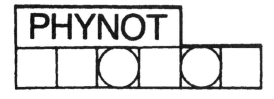

PHYNOT

Oh, Edna--I can't get in

WHAT DO YOU CALL
AN OFFICER WHO
LOST THE KEY
TO HIS HOUSE?

Now arrange the circled letters to form the surprise answer, as suggested by the above cartoon.

Print answer here A " ◯◯◯ ◯◯◯ "

JUMBLE

Unscramble these four Jumbles, one letter to each square, to form four ordinary words.

PUPER
◯◯◯◯◯

HORTT
◯◯◯◯◯

GAIMBY
◯◯◯◯◯◯

UMPING
◯◯◯◯◯◯

Say, George--I'm a little short

WHAT HE DID WHEN HE RAN INTO HIS PAL.

Now arrange the circled letters to form the surprise answer, as suggested by the above cartoon.

Print answer here ◯◯◯ THE ◯◯◯◯◯ ON ◯◯◯

JUMBLE®

Unscramble these four Jumbles, one letter to each square, to form four ordinary words.

NAHVE

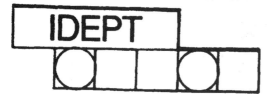

IDEPT

DRENGE

YULOHN

They can afford it

PENTHOUSE DWELLERS USUALLY PAY THIS.

Now arrange the circled letters to form the surprise answer, as suggested by the above cartoon.

Print answer here

JUMBLE®

Unscramble these four Jumbles, one letter to each square, to form four ordinary words.

VENET

ROFOL

FLUIFT

KENART

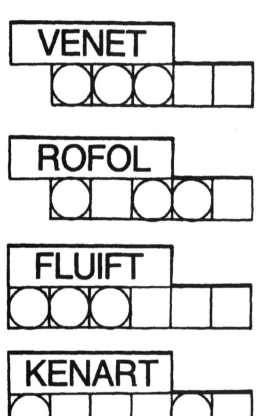

ONE OF THE IDENTICAL TWINS WAS FIVE FEET TALL — WHAT WAS THE OTHER?

Now arrange the circled letters to form the surprise answer, as suggested by the above cartoon.

Print answer here ⬡⬡⬡⬡ ⬡⬡⬡⬡⬡ , ⬡⬡⬡

64

JUMBLE®

Unscramble these four Jumbles, one letter to each square, to form four ordinary words.

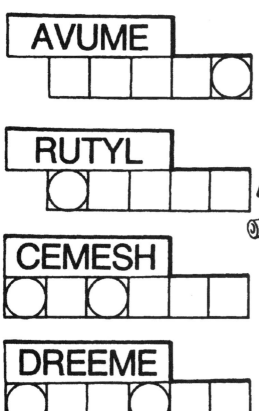

AVUME

RUTYL

CEMESH

DREEME

Junior wants to go along

JUST MARRIED

PEOPLE IN LOVE
SELDOM TRAVEL
IN THESE.

Now arrange the circled letters to form the surprise answer, as suggested by the above cartoon.

Print answer here

JUMBLE®

Unscramble these four Jumbles, one letter to each square, to form four ordinary words.

USEED

CILLA

TAIROD

YARRIT

WHAT SOME PEOPLE TRAVEL IN WHILE REMAINING AT HOME.

Now arrange the circled letters to form the surprise answer, as suggested by the above cartoon.

Print answer here

JUMBLE®

Unscramble these four Jumbles, one letter to each square, to form four ordinary words.

WABLY

UPSIO

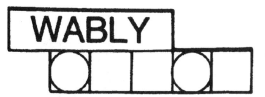

RIGLYM

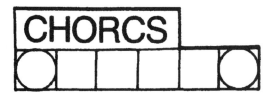

CHORCS

This'll make Page One!

WHAT A CRIME WAVE GETS IN THE NEWSPAPER.

Now arrange the circled letters to form the surprise answer, as suggested by the above cartoon.

Print answer here A ⃝⃝⃝ ⃝⃝⃝⃝⃝⃝⃝

JUMBLE®

Unscramble these four Jumbles, one letter to each square, to form four ordinary words.

YERNT

TACCH

SITMIF

HEELAX

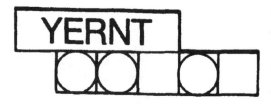

Can't wait to get home into those friendly slippers

HIGH HEELS CAN OFTEN BE THIS.

Now arrange the circled letters to form the surprise answer, as suggested by the above cartoon.

Print answer here " ☐☐☐☐ " ☐☐☐☐☐☐☐

JUMBLE®

Unscramble these four Jumbles, one letter to each square, to form four ordinary words.

KLANF

POSOW

FLAUDE

MOUPID

IN THE THEATER, THESE MEAN NO WORK AND NO PLAY.

Now arrange the circled letters to form the surprise answer, as suggested by the above cartoon.

Print answer here

JUMBLE.

Unscramble these four Jumbles, one letter to each square, to form four ordinary words.

WANTY

CEIPE

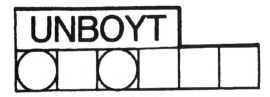

UNBOYT

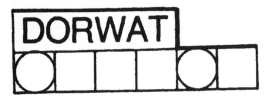

DORWAT

WHAT THE UMPIRE TURNED PIZZA CHEF ANNOUNCED.

Now arrange the circled letters to form the surprise answer, as suggested by the above cartoon.

Print answer here

JUMBLE®

Unscramble these four Jumbles, one letter to each square, to form four ordinary words.

YITED

TAVIL

FARREY

NEXTTE

HIS BUSINESS SUCCESS DEPENDS ON DRIVING CUSTOMERS AWAY.

Now arrange the circled letters to form the surprise answer, as suggested by the above cartoon.

Print answer here A ⬡⬡⬡⬡ ⬡⬡⬡⬡⬡⬡

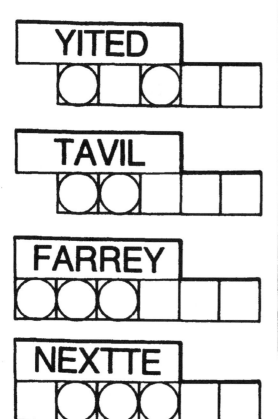

JUMBLE®

Unscramble these four Jumbles, one letter to each square, to form four ordinary words.

HUVOC

DAGLE

GRATTE

SOARUE

WHAT THE LUMBERJACK WENT DOWNSTREAM ON.

Now arrange the circled letters to form the surprise answer, as suggested by the above cartoon.

Print answer here A " ◯◯◯◯◯◯◯◯ "

JUMBLE®

Unscramble these four Jumbles, one letter to each square, to form four ordinary words.

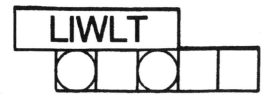

LIWLT

AMLET

COASIF

NAHLED

WHAT A DEEP-SEA DIVER MUST DO WHEN HE HAS A PROBLEM.

Now arrange the circled letters to form the surprise answer, as suggested by the above cartoon.

Print answer here

JUMBLE®

Unscramble these four Jumbles, one letter to each square, to form four ordinary words.

WERFE

GLIYN

HERNUT

BOADUN

WHAT DO YOU CALL A HUMORIST WITH A SPLIT PERSONALITY?

Now arrange the circled letters to form the surprise answer, as suggested by the above cartoon.

Print answer here A

JUMBLE®

Unscramble these four Jumbles, one letter to each square, to form four ordinary words.

NEPEC

TURTE

DEBALF

GIFFEY

WHAT THE NEW OWNER OF THE RUN-DOWN STEAK HOUSE TRIED TO DO.

Now arrange the circled letters to form the surprise answer, as suggested by the above cartoon.

Print answer here

JUMBLE®

Unscramble these four Jumbles, one letter to
each square, to form four ordinary words.

LIQUA

CLOIG

RAKNEC

TALCOE

We're unique

WHAT THE CAMERA
CLUB MEMBERS
CALLED THEM-
SELVES.

Now arrange the circled letters to form the
surprise answer, as suggested by the above
cartoon.

*Print answer
here* A

JUMBLE®

Unscramble these four Jumbles, one letter to each square, to form four ordinary words.

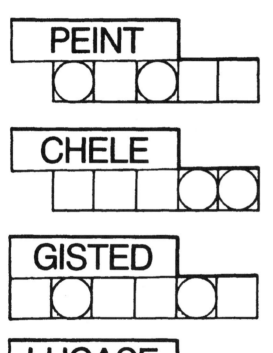

PEINT

CHELE

GISTED

LUCASE

THE FLAW IN THE BUTCHER'S GOLF GAME.

Now arrange the circled letters to form the surprise answer, as suggested by the above cartoon.

Print answer here

JUMBLE®

Unscramble these four Jumbles, one letter to
each square, to form four ordinary words.

NOMUD

HECEK

DOMBEY

VEEBAH

HOW THE LAZY
GARDENER FELT
ABOUT HIS WORK.

Now arrange the circled letters to form the
surprise answer, as suggested by the above
cartoon.

Print answer here

JUMBLE®

Unscramble these four Jumbles, one letter to each square, to form four ordinary words.

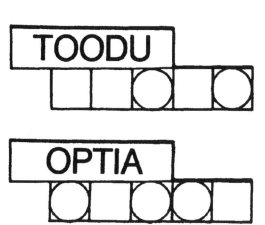

TOODU

OPTIA

VINTEN

INFREY

WHAT THE COM-
MERCIAL FISHERMAN
LIVED ON.

Now arrange the circled letters to form the surprise answer, as suggested by the above cartoon.

Print answer here

JUMBLE®

Unscramble these four Jumbles, one letter to each square, to form four ordinary words.

INGAR

FEACH

LEMOTE

ROCCEE

WHAT THE MELANCHOLY PAINTER MADE.

Now arrange the circled letters to form the surprise answer, as suggested by the above cartoon.

Print answer here

JUMBLE®

Unscramble these four Jumbles, one letter to each square, to form four ordinary words.

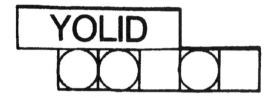
YOLID

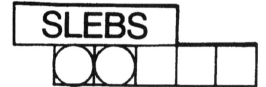
SLEBS

QUINUE

NAHZIG

WHAT THE MATADOR TURNED ROAD BUILDER LIKED MOST ABOUT HIS WORK.

Now arrange the circled letters to form the surprise answer, as suggested by the above cartoon.

Print answer here THE ◯◯◯◯◯◯◯◯◯◯◯◯

JUMBLE®

Unscramble these four Jumbles, one letter to each square, to form four ordinary words.

KAYLE

TIPAL

GANDEA

HENBID

THIS CAN TURN A SHOE INTO A SLIPPER.

Now arrange the circled letters to form the surprise answer, as suggested by the above cartoon.

Print answer here A

JUMBLE®

Unscramble these four Jumbles, one letter to
each square, to form four ordinary words.

LUTEL

NONAY

TIPOCE

KNABIG

Okay,
I'm in

BIRDS AND COM-
PUTER BUFFS
ARE BOTH COM-
FORTABLE
WITH THIS.

Now arrange the circled letters to form the
surprise answer, as suggested by the above
cartoon.

***Print answer
here*** ⭕⭕⭕⭕⭕ ON ⭕⭕⭕⭕

JUMBLE

Unscramble these four Jumbles, one letter to each square, to form four ordinary words.

CANKS

SYSEM

WOTOWK

BENZAR

He'll be working the midnight shift tomorrow

WHAT THE BORED REPORTER ENDED UP WITH.

Now arrange the circled letters to form the surprise answer, as suggested by the above cartoon.

Print answer here

A

JUMBLE®

Unscramble these four Jumbles, one letter to each square, to form four ordinary words.

CHACO

FREVE

LARTEY

YONIFT

I can't see around them

They're so big

TRUCKS CREATE THIS WHEREVER THEY GO.

Now arrange the circled letters to form the surprise answer, as suggested by the above cartoon.

Print answer here

" ⬡⬡⬡⬡⬡ " ⬡⬡⬡⬡⬡⬡⬡⬡

JUMBLE®

Unscramble these four Jumbles, one letter to each square, to form four ordinary words.

HURCS

GYKAW

CHOSOL

TREFFO

All set

... and action

A GOOD CAMERA-
MAN WILL
DO THIS.

Now arrange the circled letters to form the surprise answer, as suggested by the above cartoon.

Print answer here ⬡⬡⬡⬡⬡⬡ **ON HIS** ⬡⬡⬡⬡⬡

JUMBLE®

Unscramble these four Jumbles, one letter to each square, to form four ordinary words.

VALIE

NAKOE

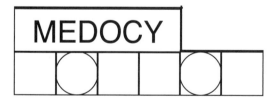

RAHGEC

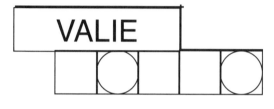

MEDOCY

Haven't been this relaxed in a long time

It's so peaceful

HOW THEIR FIRST VACATION IN YEARS MADE THEM FEEL.

Now arrange the circled letters to form the surprise answer, as suggested by the above cartoon.

Print answer here " 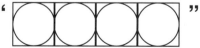 "

JUMBLE

Unscramble these four Jumbles, one letter to
each square, to form four ordinary words.

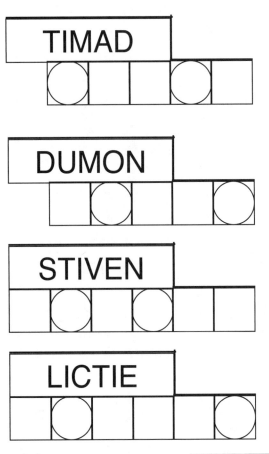

TIMAD

DUMON

STIVEN

LICTIE

Hello, I'm calling for
Ajax Roofing, and ...

CLICK!

Hello?
Hello?

OFTEN HEARD BY
A PHONE SOLICI-
TOR IN THE
MIDDLE OF THE
MESSAGE.

Now arrange the circled letters to form the
surprise answer, as suggested by the above
cartoon.

*Print answer
here*

THE

JUMBLE®

Unscramble these four Jumbles, one letter to each square, to form four ordinary words.

GITHE

TRAFC

HILUME

GAIWHE

EXCESS CALORIES CAN TURN INTO THIS.

Now arrange the circled letters to form the surprise answer, as suggested by the above cartoon.

Print answer here A

JUMBLE®

Unscramble these four Jumbles, one letter to each square, to form four ordinary words.

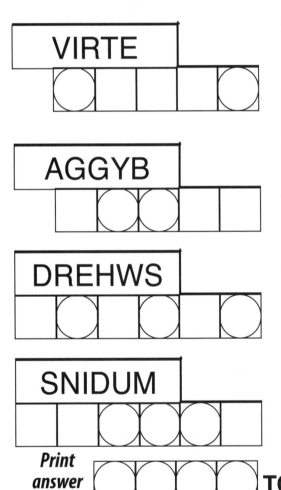

VIRTE

AGGYB

DREHWS

SNIDUM

The percentile in the fourth quadrant ...

Got any bicarbonate?

AN AFTER-DINNER SPEAKER'S REMARKS CAN BECOME THIS.

Now arrange the circled letters to form the surprise answer, as suggested by the above cartoon.

Print answer here ☐☐☐☐ TO ☐☐☐☐☐☐☐

JUMBLE®

Unscramble these four Jumbles, one letter to each square, to form four ordinary words.

KIHCT

DULGI

LEMOTE

DORNEV

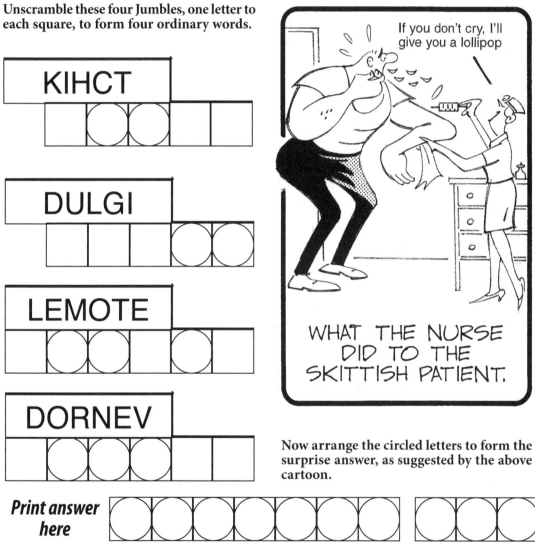

If you don't cry, I'll give you a lollipop

WHAT THE NURSE DID TO THE SKITTISH PATIENT.

Now arrange the circled letters to form the surprise answer, as suggested by the above cartoon.

Print answer here

JUMBLE®

Unscramble these four Jumbles, one letter to
each square, to form four ordinary words.

TOODU

FETHY

GUYSAR

YECKAL

AIR POLLUTION
DOES THIS.

Now arrange the circled letters to form the
surprise answer, as suggested by the above
cartoon.

**Print
answer
here** NO ☐☐☐☐☐☐☐☐ ☐☐☐☐☐

JUMBLE®

Unscramble these four Jumbles, one letter to each square, to form four ordinary words.

RYRUH

ASSOB

GOTTOR

SERVTY

Hey, that's real cool, man

THE KIDS SAID THE OLD FASH-IONED RECORD WAS ---

Now arrange the circled letters to form the surprise answer, as suggested by the above cartoon.

Print answer here

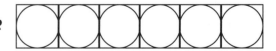

JUMBLE®

Unscramble these four Jumbles, one letter to each square, to form four ordinary words.

TELIE

CLUNE

LIFRAY

FAERRY

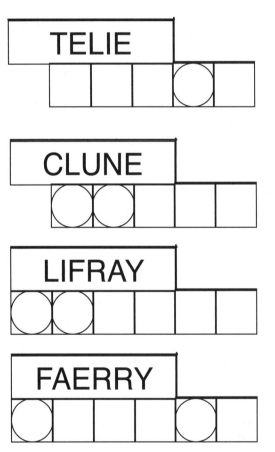

Hold tight

Eek -- I'm getting soaked

A WHITE WATER ADVENTURE USUALLY BECOMES THIS.

Now arrange the circled letters to form the surprise answer, as suggested by the above cartoon.

Print answer here **A** 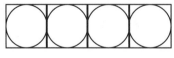 **OF**

JUMBLE®

Unscramble these four Jumbles, one letter to each square, to form four ordinary words.

MARFE

YAPEE

BLARGE

BLOUFE

I'll sue!

Oops -- sorry, sir

WHAT YOU MIGHT CALL THE DINER'S THREAT AT THE STEAKHOUSE.

Now arrange the circled letters to form the surprise answer, as suggested by the above cartoon.

Print answer here A

JUMBLE®

Unscramble these four Jumbles, one letter to each square, to form four ordinary words.

TYTID

CNOTH

FISHAM

GISTED

Hey, this makes me look fat

WHY SHE DIDN'T BUY THE SWIMSUIT.

Now arrange the circled letters to form the surprise answer, as suggested by the above cartoon.

Print answer here

JUMBLE®

Unscramble these four Jumbles, one letter to
each square, to form four ordinary words.

TEWCI

WOPOH

MOSHAN

RESPON

WHY THE FORTUNE
TELLERS DID NOT
ATTEND THE
CHARITY DINNER.

Now arrange the circled letters to form the
surprise answer, as suggested by the above
cartoon.

*Print
answer* **IT WAS** ⬡⬡⬡ - ⬡⬡⬡⬡⬡⬡⬡
here

JUMBLE®

Unscramble these four Jumbles, one letter to each square, to form four ordinary words.

LEWJE

LOCON

TRARAT

DIRAHS

His lectures never leave us up in the clouds

WHAT THE STU-DENTS CONSIDERED THE GEOLOGY PROFESSOR.

Now arrange the circled letters to form the surprise answer, as suggested by the above cartoon.

Print answer here TO

JUMBLE®

Unscramble these four Jumbles, one letter to each square, to form four ordinary words.

TORNS

PIDEB

IMUSSE

LOOSAN

Better and better

HOW THE GIFTED BALLET STUDENT MEASURED HER PROGRESS.

Now arrange the circled letters to form the surprise answer, as suggested by the above cartoon.

Print answer here **BY** ⬡⬡⬡⬡⬡ **AND** ⬡⬡⬡⬡⬡⬡⬡

JUMBLE®

Unscramble these four Jumbles, one letter to each square, to form four ordinary words.

EAGAD

BASAH

OCCRAD

FRUIGE

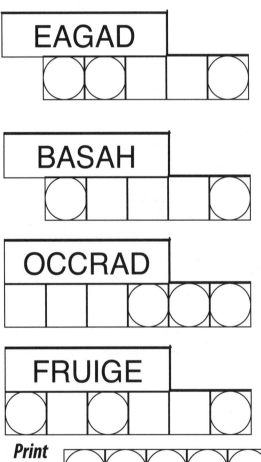

It's almost midnight

One more batch to go

WHAT THE BUSY COUNTERFEITER DID.

Now arrange the circled letters to form the surprise answer, as suggested by the above cartoon.

Print answer here

100

JUMBLE®

Unscramble these four Jumbles, one letter to each square, to form four ordinary words.

RUHTT

CRAFS

TALOZE

RAPHEC

A BARBER'S
SHAVING SKILLS
MUST BE THIS.

Now arrange the circled letters to form the surprise answer, as suggested by the above cartoon.

Print answer here

JUMBLE®

Unscramble these four Jumbles, one letter to each square, to form four ordinary words.

FLONE

CREDY

BORREK

ROSIAL

We missed you

WHEN MOM RE-
TURNED FROM A
BUSINESS TRIP
SHE WAS ---

Now arrange the circled letters to form the surprise answer, as suggested by the above cartoon.

Print answer here ⬡⬡⬡⬡⬡ **IN THE** " ⬡⬡⬡⬡⬡ "

JUMBLE®

Unscramble these four Jumbles, one letter to each square, to form four ordinary words.

NEKIF

GULAH

THORAU

PLOARE

I'm leveling off at 75,000 feet

That's a new record

AN EXPERIENCED PILOT CAN END UP HERE.

Now arrange the circled letters to form the surprise answer, as suggested by the above cartoon.

Print answer here **ON A** ☐☐☐☐☐☐☐ ☐☐☐☐☐☐

JUMBLE®

Unscramble these four Jumbles, one letter to
each square, to form four ordinary words.

KIHCC

EGGRO

DMAAMN

TUFITO

It's my secret formula

Real brainy guy

WHAT A BEER
BREWER NEEDS.

Now arrange the circled letters to form the
surprise answer, as suggested by the above
cartoon.

Print answer here A ☐☐☐☐ ☐☐☐ **IT**

JUMBLE®

Unscramble these four Jumbles, one letter to each square, to form four ordinary words.

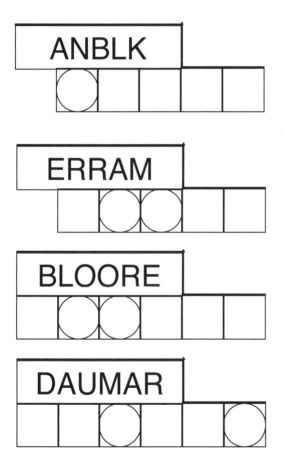

ANBLK

ERRAM

BLOORE

DAUMAR

Oh, yeah? Yeah! It's getting tougher and tougher

UNION TALKS OFTEN BECOME THIS.

Now arrange the circled letters to form the surprise answer, as suggested by the above cartoon.

Print answer here

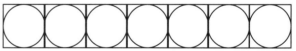

105

JUMBLE®

Unscramble these four Jumbles, one letter to each square, to form four ordinary words.

RUYLS

BLAYK

LEEXUD

AIBBED

I'm having such a good time

A COUPLE OF GLASSES OF CHAMPAGNE CAN LEAVE YOU LIKE THIS.

Now arrange the circled letters to form the surprise answer, as suggested by the above cartoon.

Print answer here

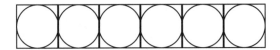

JUMBLE

Unscramble these four Jumbles, one letter to
each square, to form four ordinary words.

VARAL

VOCEL

GLEANT

NEMDIP

HOW DO HOBOS
GET ABOUT?

Now arrange the circled letters to form the
surprise answer, as suggested by the above
cartoon.

**Print
answer THEY**
here

JUMBLE®

Unscramble these four Jumbles, one letter to each square, to form four ordinary words.

LEERD

TOAQU

VOCENX

HUBELS

He can use the practice

A BARBER WHO TRIMS HIS OWN HAIR DOES THIS.

Now arrange the circled letters to form the surprise answer, as suggested by the above cartoon.

Print answer here

JUMBLE®

Unscramble these four Jumbles, one letter to each square, to form four ordinary words.

PAROE

BISCA

SOLANG

RITHEH

Did you read my new theory?

Very astute concept

WHAT THE PRO-
FESSORS TURNED
THE ISLAND
CRUISE INTO.

Now arrange the circled letters to form the surprise answer, as suggested by the above cartoon.

Print answer here

A

JUMBLE®

Unscramble these four Jumbles, one letter to
each square, to form four ordinary words.

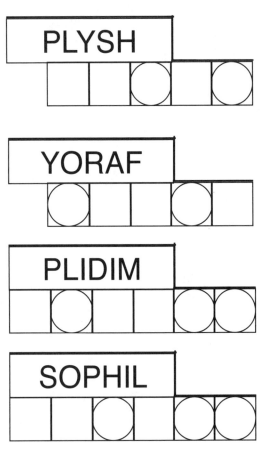

PLYSH

YORAF

PLIDIM

SOPHIL

It's all
yours

WHY HE SOLD
THE GARBAGE
DUMP.

Now arrange the circled letters to form the
surprise answer, as suggested by the above
cartoon.

Print answer here

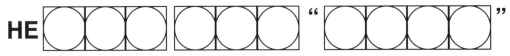

HE

JUMBLE®

Unscramble these four Jumbles, one letter to
each square, to form four ordinary words.

GEDUN

RICLY

UNDASE

GORUME

Wow!
Gorgeous!

WHAT THE
EXOTIC DANCER
FACED EVERY DAY.

Now arrange the circled letters to form the
surprise answer, as suggested by the above
cartoon.

Print answer here

THE

JUMBLE®

Unscramble these four Jumbles, one letter to each square, to form four ordinary words.

DITAU

GINOR

WHYNOA

INMALY

It'll be good for your back

How much did it cost?

HOW HUBBY TOOK IT WHEN SHE BOUGHT AN EX-PENSIVE MATTRESS.

Now arrange the circled letters to form the surprise answer, as suggested by the above cartoon.

Print answer here ◯◯◯◯◯ ◯◯◯◯

JUMBLE®

Unscramble these four Jumbles, one letter to
each square, to form four ordinary words.

NIYKK

TAING

UNBEAT

BROTED

Uh oh ... gotta
get to work

WHAT THE
FUNERAL DIRECTOR
CONSIDERED
HIS JOB.

Now arrange the circled letters to form the
surprise answer, as suggested by the above
cartoon.

Print
answer
here   AN

JUMBLE®

Unscramble these four Jumbles, one letter to each square, to form four ordinary words.

VOYCE

STURB

NERCRO

LIZZES

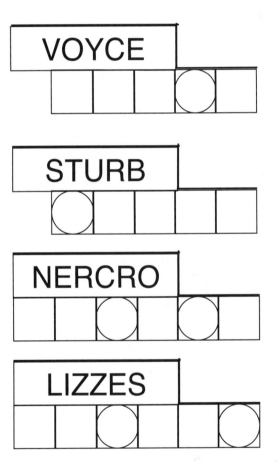

No rain, no heat, no nothin'

A BALMY DAY FORECAST CAN BE THIS.

Now arrange the circled letters to form the surprise answer, as suggested by the above cartoon.

Print answer here A " ⬡⬡⬡⬡⬡⬡ "

JUMBLE®

Unscramble these four Jumbles, one letter to each square, to form four ordinary words.

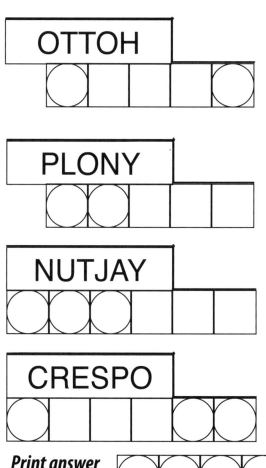

OTTOH

PLONY

NUTJAY

CRESPO

This job makes me feel wonderful

HOW THE GEORGIA FRUIT PICKER FELT AFTER A DAY'S WORK.

Now arrange the circled letters to form the surprise answer, as suggested by the above cartoon.

Print answer here

JUMBLE®

Unscramble these four Jumbles, one letter to each square, to form four ordinary words.

DESOU

LECEX

GOUTIN

LALCOW

Perfect fit

A natural for the job

YOU MIGHT SAY THE FASHION MODEL WAS THIS TO HIS WORK.

Now arrange the circled letters to form the surprise answer, as suggested by the above cartoon.

Print answer here

116

JUMBLE®

Unscramble these four Jumbles, one letter to each square, to form four ordinary words.

TAVIL

TOXEL

NEMPAN

YALTIX

It's time for your annual fiscal

WHAT THE TAX-MAN GAVE THE DOCTOR.

Now arrange the circled letters to form the surprise answer, as suggested by the above cartoon.

Print answer here

AN ⬡⬡⬡⬡⬡⬡⬡⬡⬡⬡⬡

JUMBLE®

Unscramble these four Jumbles, one letter to each square, to form four ordinary words.

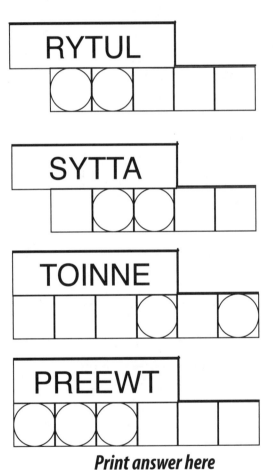

RYTUL

SYTTA

TOINNE

PREEWT

THE PRESIDENT OF AN ELECTRIC COMPANY CAN BE FOUND HERE.

Now arrange the circled letters to form the surprise answer, as suggested by the above cartoon.

Print answer here

THE ⬡⬡⬡⬡ OF " ⬡⬡⬡⬡⬡ "

JUMBLE®

Unscramble these four Jumbles, one letter to each square, to form four ordinary words.

LIVAL

SYSOM

WEEYAL

HONUKO

Aw gosh, I never get a break

WHAT SOUR GRAPES CAN TURN INTO.

Now arrange the circled letters to form the surprise answer, as suggested by the above cartoon.

Print answer here

JUMBLE

Unscramble these four Jumbles, one letter to each square, to form four ordinary words.

LAANB

VREYN

GURCOH

MESORK

Think she's good enough, sir?

A DANCER'S PER-
FORMANCE RESTS
ON THIS.

Now arrange the circled letters to form the surprise answer, as suggested by the above cartoon.

Print answer here

JUMBLE®

Unscramble these four Jumbles, one letter to each square, to form four ordinary words.

ETIRP

GUBOH

ENPOTT

GATHIL

Control those horses, I want a smooth ride

Yes, m'lord

WHAT THE KING ENDED UP WITH WHEN HE DRANK TOO MUCH.

Now arrange the circled letters to form the surprise answer, as suggested by the above cartoon.

Print answer here

A " ◯◯◯◯◯ " ◯◯◯◯◯

JUMBLE®

Unscramble these four Jumbles, one letter to each square, to form four ordinary words.

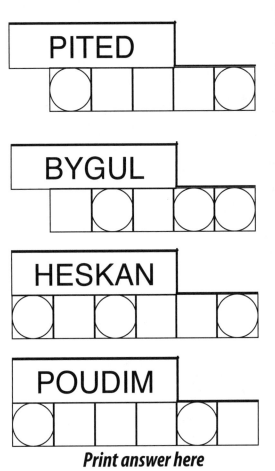

PITED

BYGUL

HESKAN

POUDIM

Print answer here

Wonderful person

Real salt of the earth

THEY THOUGHT THE COMEDIAN WAS THIS.

Now arrange the circled letters to form the surprise answer, as suggested by the above cartoon.

A " ⬭⬭⬭⬭⬭ ⬭⬭ " ⬭⬭⬭

JUMBLE®

Unscramble these four Jumbles, one letter to each square, to form four ordinary words.

RORYS

KAFLE

NUTTOB

POAFFY

You're to fly her cross-country

I quit

WHAT THE UNHAPPY PILOT DID.

Now arrange the circled letters to form the surprise answer, as suggested by the above cartoon.

Print answer here

JUMBLE®

Unscramble these four Jumbles, one letter to each square, to form four ordinary words.

LASIA

HADEA

BLUTSY

SEEBID

My plan calls for a hefty tax increase

Hey, stop

SHARED BY A BUSY POLITICIAN AND A COUNTERFEITER.

Now arrange the circled letters to form the surprise answer, as suggested by the above cartoon.

Print answer here

JUMBLE®

Unscramble these four Jumbles, one letter to each square, to form four ordinary words.

ECTAN

PHRAC

ARUSSE

HERFIE

He's mine!

Leggo, I saw him first!

SOUGHT BY COM-
PETING TAXI
DRIVERS.

Now arrange the circled letters to form the surprise answer, as suggested by the above cartoon.

Print answer here

THEIR

JUMBLE®

Unscramble these four Jumbles, one letter to each square, to form four ordinary words.

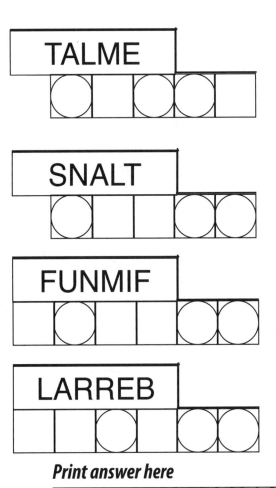

TALME

SNALT

FUNMIF

LARREB

WHAT THE ORGANIST WAS TO THE MARRIAGE CEREMONY.

Now arrange the circled letters to form the surprise answer, as suggested by the above cartoon.

Print answer here

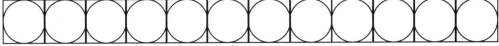

JUMBLE®

Unscramble these four Jumbles, one letter to each square, to form four ordinary words.

YERFO

CUTHE

BETASK

EBONGE

WHY THE COP DIDN'T JOIN THE NEIGHBOR-HOOD PARTY.

Now arrange the circled letters to form the surprise answer, as suggested by the above cartoon.

Print answer here

THE

JUMBLE®

Unscramble these four Jumbles, one letter to
each square, to form four ordinary words.

IXTYS

ASTEE

DRENGE

TRAIPY

Really
covers the
ground

IMPORTANT FOR A
RACE HORSE TO
MAKE DURING
TRAINING.

Print answer here

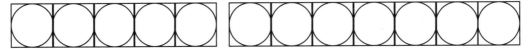

JUMBLE®

Unscramble these four Jumbles, one letter to each square, to form four ordinary words.

DORRA

YASOP

TAUMER

REESHY

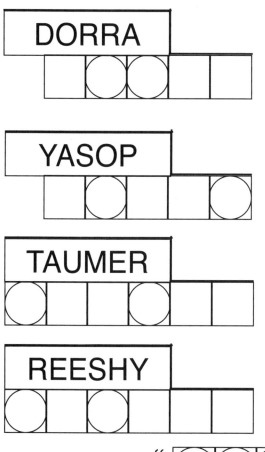

The vote was sobering

WHAT THE COMIC INDULGED IN WHEN THE TOWN BANNED LIQUOR.

Now arrange the circled letters to form the surprise answer, as suggested by the above cartoon.

Print answer here " ◯◯◯ " ◯◯◯◯◯

JUMBLE®

Unscramble these four Jumbles, one letter to
each square, to form four ordinary words.

EGUSS

BALFE

INLATE

WAHLIE

Tell them no. Same
old boring people

THE MOVIE STAR
AVOIDED THE
PARTY BECAUSE
SHE WAS ---

Now arrange the circled letters to form the
surprise answer, as suggested by the above
cartoon.

Print answer here ◯◯◯◯ - ◯◯◯◯

JUMBLE®

Unscramble these four Jumbles, one letter to each square, to form four ordinary words.

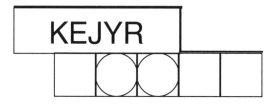

KEJYR

FOTOA

VERROF

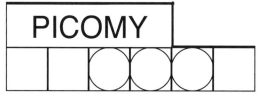

PICOMY

It must be nice to be the boss's kid

WHAT THE CHIEF'S SON WAS.

Now arrange the circled letters to form the surprise answer, as suggested by the above cartoon.

Print answer here "  "

JUMBLE®

Unscramble these four Jumbles, one letter to each square, to form four ordinary words.

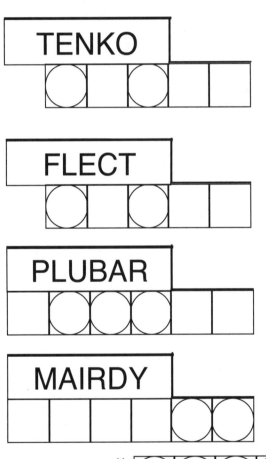

TENKO

FLECT

PLUBAR

MAIRDY

She's coming in!

At least 200 %#!&@ barrels a day

WHAT THE VISI-TORS HEARD AT THE OIL WELL.

Now arrange the circled letters to form the surprise answer, as suggested by the above cartoon.

Print answer here "⬡⬡⬡⬡⬡⬡" ⬡⬡⬡⬡⬡

JUMBLE®

Unscramble these four Jumbles, one letter to each square, to form four ordinary words.

NELLK

PUJEL

FAYLBB

DORIAH

Not interested

No obligation of any kind

OFFERED BY A SHADY TELE-MARKETER.

Now arrange the circled letters to form the surprise answer, as suggested by the above cartoon.

Print answer here

A " ⬡⬡⬡⬡⬡ - ⬡ " ⬡⬡⬡⬡

JUMBLE

Unscramble these four Jumbles, one letter to
each square, to form four ordinary words.

TURET

GERME

RUSTYD

BROJEB

You call this a steak?!

WHAT HE CON-
SIDERED THE
WAITER'S
RECOMMENDATION.

Now arrange the circled letters to form the
surprise answer, as suggested by the above
cartoon.

Print answer here **A** ⬡⬡⬡ ⬡⬡⬡⬡⬡⬡

JUMBLE®

Unscramble these four Jumbles, one letter to each square, to form four ordinary words.

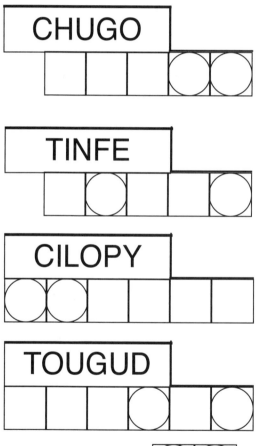

CHUGO

TINFE

CILOPY

TOUGUD

Sorry, madam, it's too late for a return

I demand to see the manager

A GOOD WAY TO GET TO THE BOTTOM OF THINGS.

Now arrange the circled letters to form the surprise answer, as suggested by the above cartoon.

Print answer here

JUMBLE®

Unscramble these four Jumbles, one letter to each square, to form four ordinary words.

GNAAP
◯◯◯◯◯

GLOIN
◯◯◯◯◯

RIQUMS
◯◯◯◯◯◯

GRIINF
◯◯◯◯◯

Yoo hoo

FOR PITCHERS, PRE-SEASON TRAINING BE-GINS WITH THIS.

Now arrange the circled letters to form the surprise answer, as suggested by the above cartoon.

Print answer here

A ◯◯◯◯◯◯ ◯◯◯◯◯

JUMBLE®

Unscramble these four Jumbles, one letter to each square, to form four ordinary words.

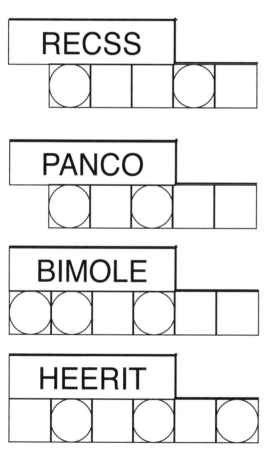

RECSS

PANCO

BIMOLE

HEERIT

Can I have the prize?

WHAT THE PRO-GRAMMER FOUND AT THE BOTTOM OF HIS SNACK BAG.

Now arrange the circled letters to form the surprise answer, as suggested by the above cartoon.

Print answer here

JUMBLE®

Unscramble these four Jumbles, one letter to each square, to form four ordinary words.

NAWTY

WHART

CODEED

HATTUG

It's your turn. She's wet

WAHH!

MOM AND HER NEWBORN BOTH NEEDED THIS.

Now arrange the circled letters to form the surprise answer, as suggested by the above cartoon.

Print answer here **A**

JUMBLE®

Unscramble these four Jumbles, one letter to each square, to form four ordinary words.

FIRGE

RAIFE

LARPIL

DYNKIL

Round trip is $450

Is that your lowest price?

SOUGHT BY AIR-LINE PASSENGERS.

Now arrange the circled letters to form the surprise answer, as suggested by the above cartoon.

Print answer here   A " ⬭⬭⬭⬭⬭ " ⬭⬭⬭⬭

JUMBLE®

Unscramble these four Jumbles, one letter to each square, to form four ordinary words.

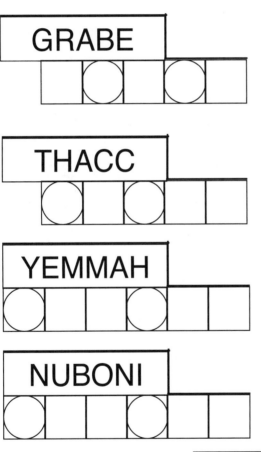

GRABE

THACC

YEMMAH

NUBONI

Another left

THIS WILL FIRE UP A BOXING CROWD.

Now arrange the circled letters to form the surprise answer, as suggested by the above cartoon.

Print answer here A

140

JUMBLE®

Unscramble these four Jumbles, one letter to each square, to form four ordinary words.

HARBO

DISAT

UPCHIC

UNROAD

You have the figure for it

$5,000

WHAT IT TAKES TO WEAR THE LATEST FASHION.

Now arrange the circled letters to form the surprise answer, as suggested by the above cartoon.

Print answer here

A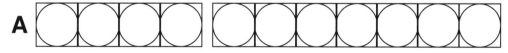

JUMBLE®

Unscramble these four Jumbles, one letter to
each square, to form four ordinary words.

TRYAR

CUHDY

SNODEC

NESING

That's Uncle Bob. We
don't discuss him

WHERE THE CROOK APPEARED ON THE FAMILY TREE.

Now arrange the circled letters to form the
surprise answer, as suggested by the above
cartoon.

Print
answer
here

ON THE ☐☐☐☐☐ ☐☐☐☐☐

JUMBLE®

Unscramble these four Jumbles, one letter to each square, to form four ordinary words.

WREFE

GEFUD

FOHMAT

AIRWET

You're always late — you should be fired!

Your stop is coming up, sir

WHAT THE BUS DRIVER WANTED TO TELL THE RUDE PASSENGER.

Now arrange the circled letters to form the surprise answer, as suggested by the above cartoon.

Print answer here

☐☐☐☐☐ **TO** ☐☐☐ ☐☐☐

JUMBLE®

Unscramble these four Jumbles, one letter to each square, to form four ordinary words.

TACHY

FITEB

HURTOF

RANLEY

I won! I won!

Now I can buy that fur coat

WHEN HE HIT THE JACKPOT THE GAMBLER'S WIFE SAID HE WAS ---

Now arrange the circled letters to form the surprise answer, as suggested by the above cartoon.

Print answer here

HER " ⃝⃝⃝⃝⃝⃝ " ⃝⃝⃝⃝

JUMBLE®

Unscramble these four Jumbles, one letter to each square, to form four ordinary words.

YINCC

DUBOT

TIQUEY

CLOUNK

Next

IF YOU SUSPECT YOUR DOCTOR OF BEING A QUACK, MAYBE YOU'D BETTER DO THIS.

Now arrange the circled letters to form the surprise answer, as suggested by the above cartoon.

Print answer here

JUMBLE®

Unscramble these four Jumbles, one letter to each square, to form four ordinary words.

NOWNK

VALIA

LUTTUM

BELNAG

It's been four months and three days

HARD TO STOP WHEN YOU GIVE UP SMOKING.

Now arrange the circled letters to form the surprise answer, as suggested by the above cartoon.

Print answer here

IT

JUMBLE®

Unscramble these four Jumbles, one letter to each square, to form four ordinary words.

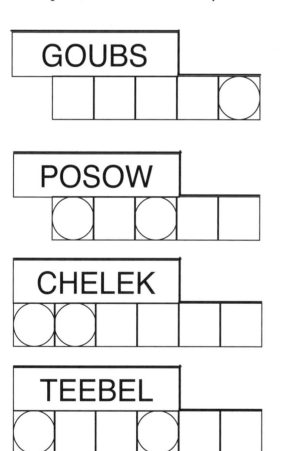

GOUBS

POSOW

CHELEK

TEEBEL

Thank you, come again

YOU MIGHT SAY EVERY SELF-EMPLOYED PERSON IS THIS.

Now arrange the circled letters to form the surprise answer, as suggested by the above cartoon.

Print answer here

JUMBLE®

Unscramble these four Jumbles, one letter to each square, to form four ordinary words.

TELIT

CEIPE

PHOCON

TAIROD

... and we'll be in the 90s all week

Everyone's complaining about it

WHAT THE FORE-CASTER ENDED UP WITH DURING THE SUMMER.

Now arrange the circled letters to form the surprise answer, as suggested by the above cartoon.

Print answer here **A**

JUMBLE®

Unscramble these four Jumbles, one letter to each square, to form four ordinary words.

ANUFA

ILLAC

BLUEBB

TREENI

Stop! Quiet down

A ROOMFUL OF FRISKY CUBS CAN BE THIS.

Now arrange the circled letters to form the surprise answer, as suggested by the above cartoon.

Print answer here

" ⬡⬡ - ⬡⬡⬡⬡⬡ - ⬡⬡⬡⬡ "

JUMBLE®

Unscramble these four Jumbles, one letter to each square, to form four ordinary words.

ROGAC

BYRIN

BIMROD

DIRTOR

This hurts

A PIECE OF
GYM EQUIPMENT
THAT CAN
CAUSE PAIN.

Now arrange the circled letters to form the surprise answer, as suggested by the above cartoon.

Print answer here   A ◯◯◯ ◯◯◯◯◯◯

JUMBLE®

Unscramble these four Jumbles, one letter to each square, to form four ordinary words.

CREMY

BOINS

NUMMAG

PINSOO

It'll take all my winnings

AJAX KEGLERS

MIGHT BE USED BY A BOWLER TO PAY FOR A DIAMOND BROOCH.

Now arrange the circled letters to form the surprise answer, as suggested by the above cartoon.

Print answer here

JUMBLE®

Unscramble these four Jumbles, one letter to each square, to form four ordinary words.

TOINX

YURST

TINNEY

FESTOF

Oh, it's so charming

IMPORTANT FOR A
PERFECT WEDDING.

Now arrange the circled letters to form the surprise answer, as suggested by the above cartoon.

Print answer here THE ⬡⬡⬡⬡⬡ ⬡⬡⬡⬡⬡

JUMBLE®

Unscramble these four Jumbles, one letter to each square, to form four ordinary words.

WYLEN

MEFAL

LUFOWE

VIYTLE

Will you marry me?

WHY THE SKYDIVER
PROPOSED IN
MID-AIR.

Now arrange the circled letters to form the surprise answer, as suggested by the above cartoon.

Print answer here

HE " ⬡⬡⬡⬡ " ⬡⬡ ⬡⬡⬡⬡

JUMBLE®

Unscramble these four Jumbles, one letter to each square, to form four ordinary words.

PIMBL

YAIRN

DILQUI

OFTROG

First we went to dinner, then dancing...

THE SECRETARY EXCELLED AT THIS.

Now arrange the circled letters to form the surprise answer, as suggested by the above cartoon.

Print answer here

JUMBLE®

Unscramble these four Jumbles, one letter to each square, to form four ordinary words.

YOOST

TARAP

VEEBAH

JENNIO

Pay strict attention to this stance

IMPORTANT FOR BALLET STUDENTS TO DO.

Now arrange the circled letters to form the surprise answer, as suggested by the above cartoon.

Print answer here **BE ON** ◯◯◯◯◯◯ ◯◯◯◯◯

JUMBLE®

Unscramble these four Jumbles, one letter to each square, to form four ordinary words.

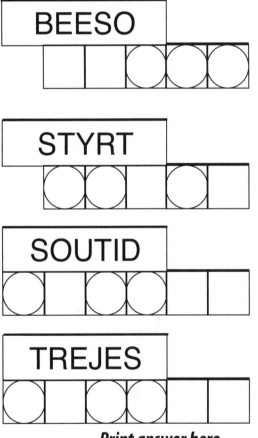

BEESO

STYRT

SOUTID

TREJES

You've ruined it. Get out!

WHAT AN INCOM-
PETENT PASTRY
CHEF SHOULD
RECEIVE.

Now arrange the circled letters to form the surprise answer, as suggested by the above cartoon.

Print answer here

HIS

JUMBLE®

Unscramble these four Jumbles, one letter to each square, to form four ordinary words.

ARICH

ENSOO

CLUDED

UNGOTE

I'm the King, let's dance

I'm the Queen, and I say let's not

They don't get along

PRODUCED BY THE SQUABBLING ROYAL COUPLE.

Now arrange the circled letters to form the surprise answer, as suggested by the above cartoon.

Print answer here

" ___ " ___

JUMBLE®

Unscramble these four Jumbles, one letter to each square, to form four ordinary words.

LIWLT

TAWLZ

SKENIC

FEINED

She looks peaceful

WHAT SHE DEVEL-
OPED WHEN SHE
TOOK UP YOGA.

Now arrange the circled letters to form the surprise answer, as suggested by the above cartoon.

Print answer here **A** ⬡⬡⬡ ⬡⬡⬡⬡⬡⬡

JUMBLE®

Unscramble these four Jumbles, one letter to each square, to form four ordinary words.

ZUZYF

UNPER

TURBAP

EXDOUT

Gotta stay in shape for the drive

WHAT THE COWBOY LIKED TO DO IN HIS SPARE TIME.

Now arrange the circled letters to form the surprise answer, as suggested by the above cartoon.

Print answer here " ⃝⃝⃝⃝ " ⃝⃝

JUMBLE®

Unscramble these four Jumbles, one letter to each square, to form four ordinary words.

SCEHS

PLUIT

MIDOWS

EXFRIP

Too much money   My carpet's ruined

WHAT THE CONDO BOARD FACED WHEN THE ROOF LEAKED.

Now arrange the circled letters to form the surprise answer, as suggested by the above cartoon.

Print answer here

A "⬡⬡⬡⬡⬡⬡⬡" ⬡⬡⬡⬡⬡

JUMBLE®

Unscramble these four Jumbles, one letter to each square, to form four ordinary words.

HELEW

YOGUN

TIENIF

THIGEY

My tummy hurts

Get dressed, you'll be fine

WHAT MOM HAD WHEN SHE DIS-MISSED HIS STOMACH-ACHE ON TEST DAY.

Now arrange the circled letters to form the surprise answer, as suggested by the above cartoon.

Print answer here

A

JUMBLE®

Unscramble these four Jumbles, one letter to each square, to form four ordinary words.

LODEY

CHOAR

CLAICO

HALNIE

I'm afraid of being hit

Talk to the shrink

WHAT THE TEAM CALLED THE SPORTS PSYCHOLOGIST.

Now arrange the circled letters to form the surprise answer, as suggested by the above cartoon.

Print answer here

THE " ☐☐☐☐ " ☐☐☐☐☐☐

Challenger Puzzles

JUMBLE®

Unscramble these six Jumbles, one letter to each square, to form six ordinary words.

LENETS

NATTIC

INDIGH

DORWYB

CORRAN

DELGEP

Let's invite all our friends

Yeah, lots of gifts

WHAT THE BRIDE AND GROOM WANTED AT THEIR NUPTIALS.

Now arrange the circled letters to form the surprise answer, as suggested by the above cartoon.

PRINT YOUR ANSWER IN THE CIRCLES BELOW

JUMBLE®

Unscramble these six Jumbles, one letter to each square, to form six ordinary words.

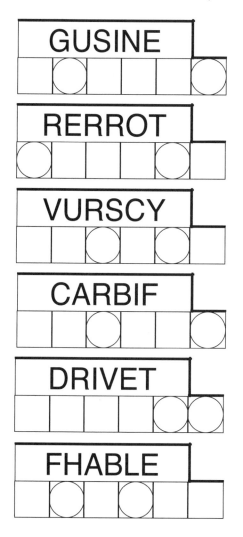

GUSINE

RERROT

VURSCY

CARBIF

DRIVET

FHABLE

He doesn't create any waste

THE BUTCHER GOT A RAISE BECAUSE HE WAS ---

Now arrange the circled letters to form the surprise answer, as suggested by the above cartoon.

PRINT YOUR ANSWER IN THE CIRCLES BELOW

A ◯◯◯◯ ◯◯◯◯◯◯ THE ◯◯◯◯

JUMBLE®

Unscramble these six Jumbles, one letter to each square, to form six ordinary words.

MYSLOB

NEUQUI

FLAGDY

GASYRS

ORTETT

HARMIO

We did it!

Now we can buy a new house

WHAT THE RETIRED COUPLE ENJOYED WHEN THEY WON THE LOTTERY.

Now arrange the circled letters to form the surprise answer, as suggested by the above cartoon.

PRINT YOUR ANSWER IN THE CIRCLES BELOW

THEIR " ⬡⬡⬡⬡⬡⬡ " ⬡⬡⬡⬡⬡

JUMBLE®

Unscramble these six Jumbles, one letter to each square, to form six ordinary words.

GYNULS

PHYNOT

CISTEB

WEABER

KOVINE

FLOSSI

Looks like a good year

Hard work but lots of peace and quiet

HE BOUGHT THE FARM BECAUSE HE WANTED THIS.

Now arrange the circled letters to form the surprise answer, as suggested by the above cartoon.

PRINT YOUR ANSWER IN THE CIRCLES BELOW

A "⬡⬡⬡⬡⬡⬡" ⬡⬡⬡⬡⬡⬡⬡⬡⬡

JUMBLE®

Unscramble these six Jumbles, one letter to each square, to form six ordinary words.

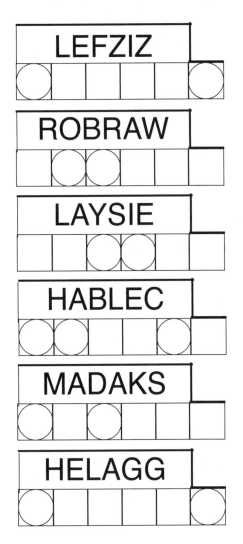

LEFZIZ

ROBRAW

LAYSIE

HABLEC

MADAKS

HELAGG

WHAT DAD DID
WHILE THE ORTHO-
DONTIST FIGURED
THE COST.

Now arrange the circled letters to form the surprise answer, as suggested by the above cartoon.

PRINT YOUR ANSWER IN THE CIRCLES BELOW

" ⬡⬡⬡⬡⬡⬡ " ⬡⬡⬡⬡⬡⬡⬡

JUMBLE®

Unscramble these six Jumbles, one letter to each square, to form six ordinary words.

NEHBID

ACOLLE

WEDDEG

CLAMBE

GOBUTH

RELUSY

She'll make us a fortune

WHY THE TIGHT-ROPE WALKER GOT THE LOAN.

Now arrange the circled letters to form the surprise answer, as suggested by the above cartoon.

PRINT YOUR ANSWER IN THE CIRCLES BELOW

◯◯◯ ◯◯◯◯◯◯◯ WAS ◯◯◯◯

JUMBLE®

Unscramble these six Jumbles, one letter to each square, to form six ordinary words.

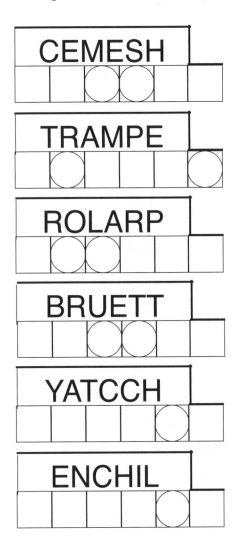

CEMESH

TRAMPE

ROLARP

BRUETT

YATCCH

ENCHIL

Tell me all about your operation

Tell me all about yours

THE KIND OF TALK THE CARDIAC PATIENTS HAD.

Now arrange the circled letters to form the surprise answer, as suggested by the above cartoon.

PRINT YOUR ANSWER IN THE CIRCLES BELOW

TO

JUMBLE

Unscramble these six Jumbles, one letter to
each square, to form six ordinary words.

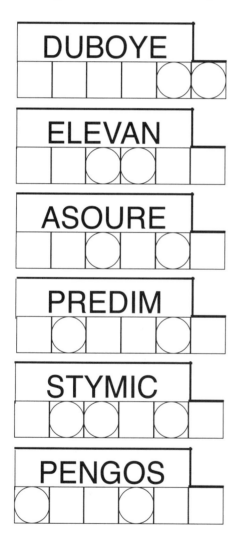

DUBOYE

ELEVAN

ASOURE

PREDIM

STYMIC

PENGOS

Everything's in full bloom

ENJOYED BY
A GARDENER.

Now arrange the circled letters to form the
surprise answer, as suggested by the above
cartoon.

PRINT YOUR ANSWER IN THE CIRCLES BELOW

JUMBLE®

Unscramble these six Jumbles, one letter to each square, to form six ordinary words.

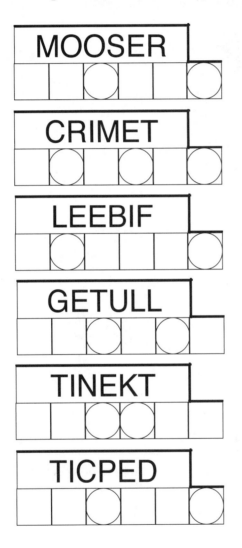

MOOSER

CRIMET

LEEBIF

GETULL

TINEKT

TICPED

He's never made a mistake

WHAT IT TAKES TO BE AN OUT-STANDING MAIL-MAN.

Now arrange the circled letters to form the surprise answer, as suggested by the above cartoon.

PRINT YOUR ANSWER IN THE CIRCLES BELOW

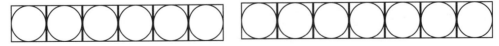

JUMBLE

Unscramble these six Jumbles, one letter to each square, to form six ordinary words.

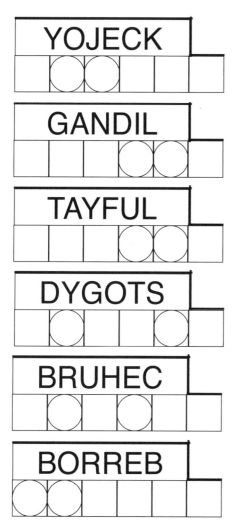

YOJECK

GANDIL

TAYFUL

DYGOTS

BRUHEC

BORREB

I've lost 4 inches off my waist

WHY SOME DIETERS TAKE PILLS.

Now arrange the circled letters to form the surprise answer, as suggested by the above cartoon.

PRINT YOUR ANSWER IN THE CIRCLES BELOW

FOR

JUMBLE.

Unscramble these six Jumbles, one letter to each square, to form six ordinary words.

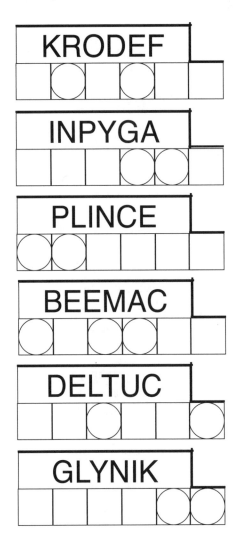

KRODEF

INPYGA

PLINCE

BEEMAC

DELTUC

GLYNIK

No playing and share the covers

WHAT THE IN-SURANCE SALES-MAN ISSUED AT BEDTIME.

Now arrange the circled letters to form the surprise answer, as suggested by the above cartoon.

PRINT YOUR ANSWER IN THE CIRCLES BELOW

A

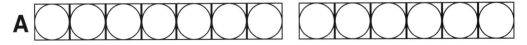

JUMBLE®

Unscramble these six Jumbles, one letter to each square, to form six ordinary words.

REMMIO

NUTHAG

FICTEN

SAQUEY

JETNUK

RICKYT

Cute

A MODEL AND HER DOG CAN BE THIS.

Now arrange the circled letters to form the surprise answer, as suggested by the above cartoon.

PRINT YOUR ANSWER IN THE CIRCLES BELOW

JUMBLE

Unscramble these six Jumbles, one letter to each square, to form six ordinary words.

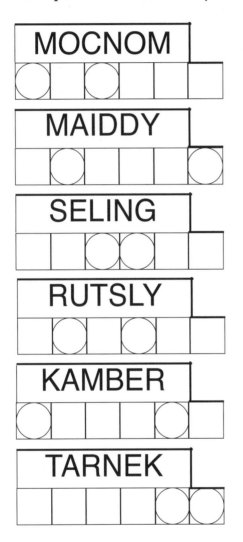

MOCNOM

MAIDDY

SELING

RUTSLY

KAMBER

TARNEK

He committed the worst one ever

WHAT THEY ENDED UP WITH WHEN THEY CLEANED THE 100-YEAR-OLD JAILHOUSE.

Now arrange the circled letters to form the surprise answer, as suggested by the above cartoon.

PRINT YOUR ANSWER IN THE CIRCLES BELOW

THE ⬡⬡⬡⬡⬡⬡ OF THE ⬡⬡⬡⬡⬡⬡⬡⬡

JUMBLE®

Unscramble these six Jumbles, one letter to
each square, to form six ordinary words.

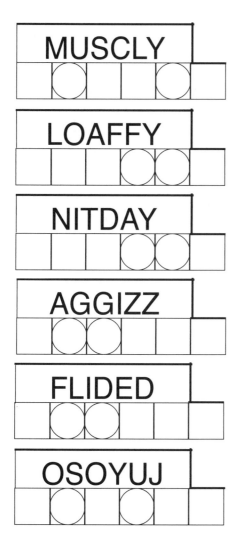

MUSCLY

LOAFFY

NITDAY

AGGIZZ

FLIDED

OSOYUJ

At least I'm
not in pain

PRACTICAL SHOES
PUT HER HERE AT
THE FORMAL DANCE.

Now arrange the circled letters to form the
surprise answer, as suggested by the above
cartoon.

PRINT YOUR ANSWER IN THE CIRCLES BELOW

ON ◯◯◯◯◯◯ ◯◯◯◯◯◯◯

JUMBLE®

Unscramble these six Jumbles, one letter to each square, to form six ordinary words.

WORMAR

RUIPFY

RAYATS

ONABBO

GLUEDE

CEEDIT

What about the grass?

Can't you see I'm resting?

ON HIS DAY OFF "WORK" CAN BE THIS TO A COUCH POTATO.

Now arrange the circled letters to form the surprise answer, as suggested by the above cartoon.

PRINT YOUR ANSWER IN THE CIRCLES BELOW

A ⬡⬡⬡⬡⬡ - ⬡⬡⬡⬡⬡⬡⬡ ⬡⬡⬡⬡

JUMBLE®

Unscramble these six Jumbles, one letter to each square, to form six ordinary words.

YIMWAD

GLEENT

VINTER

YORCUT

ANNAAB

ENVORG

WHAT HER FLOWER BED BECAME WHEN SHE WON THE CONTEST.

Now arrange the circled letters to form the surprise answer, as suggested by the above cartoon.

PRINT YOUR ANSWER IN THE CIRCLES BELOW

A ⭕⭕⭕⭕⭕⭕⭕ ⭕⭕⭕⭕⭕⭕⭕

JUMBLE®

Unscramble these six Jumbles, one letter to each square, to form six ordinary words.

URBAUN

PARULL

MALEYS

GARSIT

AVGASE

NOIDIE

Her father's the conductor

HOW THE HARPIST GOT THE LUCRA-TIVE BOOKING.

Now arrange the circled letters to form the surprise answer, as suggested by the above cartoon.

PRINT YOUR ANSWER IN THE CIRCLES BELOW

SHE ⬡⬡⬡⬡⬡⬡ ⬡⬡⬡⬡⬡⬡⬡

JUMBLE®

Unscramble these six Jumbles, one letter to each square, to form six ordinary words.

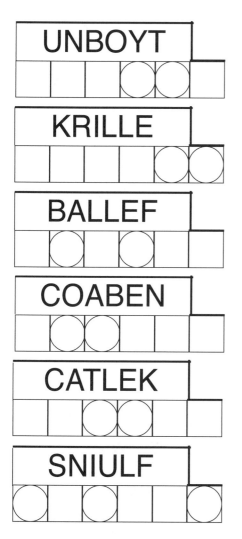

UNBOYT

KRILLE

BALLEF

COABEN

CATLEK

SNIULF

Small price increase

HOW HE FELT WHEN HE GOT HIS LAUNDRY BILL.

Now arrange the circled letters to form the surprise answer, as suggested by the above cartoon.

PRINT YOUR ANSWER IN THE CIRCLES BELOW

TO THE

JUMBLE®

Unscramble these six Jumbles, one letter to each square, to form six ordinary words.

CLUMON

ENBLIM

LADRIA

SMURTI

SABDUR

CELEEF

I'm staying indoors, it's too nice outside

THE PROFESSOR SKIPPED CLASSES BECAUSE HE WAS ——

Now arrange the circled letters to form the surprise answer, as suggested by the above cartoon.

PRINT YOUR ANSWER IN THE CIRCLES BELOW

JUMBLE

Unscramble these six Jumbles, one letter to
each square, to form six ordinary words.

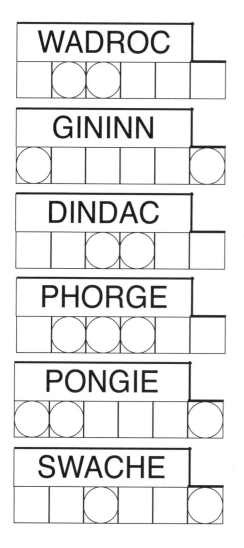

WADROC

GININN

DINDAC

PHORGE

PONGIE

SWACHE

GLASS

WHERE YOU MIGHT
END UP AFTER
YOUR KID HITS A
HOME RUN.

Now arrange the circled letters to form the
surprise answer, as suggested by the above
cartoon.

PRINT YOUR ANSWER IN THE CIRCLES BELOW

ANSWERS

1. **Jumbles:** THINK FENCE GIMLET CRAVAT
   Answer: Don't expect someone to talk turkey who's this—CHICKEN

2. **Jumbles:** LEAVE PRIOR SPONGE POORLY
   Answer: If you think golf is only a rich man's game, look at these—ALL THE POOR PLAYERS

3. **Jumbles:** FUDGE GUESS THWART OBLIGE
   Answer: What some work in the garden can leave one—"BUSHED"

4. **Jumbles:** ENTRY RAPID MYSELF THRASH
   Answer: What the guy who ignored his wife when she suggested that they buy a second car turned out to be—A PEDESTRIAN

5. **Jumbles:** BLOOD YOUNG LAWYER VELVET
   Answer: What his curly hair was beginning to do—WAVE GOOD-BYE

6. **Jumbles:** VIGIL NEWLY CATNIP BANANA
   Answer: What the archer was—"BENT" ON WINNING

7. **Jumbles:** TARRY METAL HAUNCH INFORM
   Answer: What a real firm makes that may go off in the heat—A "FIRE ALARM"

8. **Jumbles:** NOOSE ROACH POWDER TREATY
   Answer: A mistake found in terrorism—"ERROR"

9. **Jumbles:** BLOOM HANDY ADJUST IMPUTE
   Answer: It's a case of peas or beans—A POD

10. **Jumbles:** JUMBO COCOA MATRON LIZARD
    Answer: Another name for Dracula—BLOOD COUNT

11. **Jumbles:** COACH POKER STYLUS HEREBY
    Answer: What you might have when two authors sue each other—A BOOK CASE

12. **Jumbles:** DOILY GUIDE MINGLE SADIST
    Answer: What the absent-minded hen did—MISLAID AN EGG

13. **Jumbles:** VALET BAGGY ARMORY CONVEX
    Answer: How they acted at the undertakers' annual shindig—GRAVELY

14. **Jumbles:** PRINT FUZZY OUTLET COMEDY
    Answer: Could it be a sound from a dog without a pedigree?—A "MUTT-ER"

15. **Jumbles:** GLADE PARTY AGENCY NIMBLE
    Answer: What a dentist might do about those missing teeth—"BRIDGE" THE GAP

16. **Jumbles:** MAKER NAVAL PALATE UPWARD
    Answer: Could it have been a drama about a famous fleet?—"ARMADA"

17. **Jumbles:** MAIZE SOAPY UNSOLD CAMPUS
    Answer: Music that might accompany a turkey dinner—A "YAM" SESSION

18. **Jumbles:** TRIPE HOVEL STOOGE OUTFIT
    Answer: What the guy who stole a banana gave the cops—THE SLIP

19. **Jumbles:** OCCUR KHAKI BROKEN POROUS
    Answer: How does that fisherman who tends sheep on the side make a living?—BY HOOK OR BY CROOK

20. **Jumbles:** AHEAD BLIMP CANNED HUNGRY
    Answer: If joy is the opposite of sorrow, what's the opposite of woe?—GIDDAP

21. **Jumbles:** HELLO BASIC AFFRAY CAUGHT
    Answer: What kind of a guy was that press photographer?—A FLASHY ONE

22. **Jumbles:** TONIC STOOP POISON COUSIN
    Answer: Everything you should know about entrances and exits—THE INS & OUTS

23. **Jumbles:** GROIN BERTH HOOKED STOLEN
    Answer: What he was, after he bought her that big diamond—STONE-BROKE

24. **Jumbles:** LOVER FLAME POLITE MISLAY
    Answer: He works out the problems of "mixed-up" lovers—"SOLVER"

25. **Jumbles:** TRILL BOUND GOVERN ROBBER
    Answer: What the locksmith made when his shop caught fire—A BOLT FOR THE DOOR

26. **Jumbles:** GULCH HUMID FRIEZE SINGLE
    Answer: The soprano stood on the balcony so she could do this—SING "HIGHER"

27. **Jumbles:** FIFTY GROUP INNING VERIFY
    Answer: He's always forgetting, but never this—"FOR GIVING"

28. **Jumbles:** ALIAS EMBER LOCALE SUCKLE
    Answer: How much did a belt used to cost?—LESS THAN A "BUCK-LE"

29. **Jumbles:** BLAZE CLOAK LUNACY PACKET
    Answer: What it takes to have no eyebrows—A LOT OF PLUCK

30. **Jumbles:** EMPTY DAISY BODICE VIRILE
    Answer: Their relative who was known for his stinginess must have been this—VERY "CLOSE"

31. **Jumbles:** TIGER FACET BANDIT SCORCH
    Answer: If you want to relax at dinner, take this before each meal—A CHAIR

32. **Jumbles:** CHIME PANSY FLEECE TRICKY
    Answer: Might be enough to turn your hair white suddenly—LATHER

33. **Jumbles:** RANCH DICED BUTTON CRAFTY
    Answer: You can draw this as long as you live—YOUR BREATH

34. **Jumbles:** CHAFE SMACK FROSTY USEFUL
    Answer: They sometimes hold hands at the police station—CUFFS

35. **Jumbles:** JINGO CHAIR OMELET BISECT
    Answer: People like to help him out, as soon as—HE COMES IN

36. **Jumbles:** LOUSY VISTA SINFUL BELIEF
    Answer: He said he was living in the present—"TENSE"

37. **Jumbles:** VAPOR ENJOY JAGGED BOYISH
    Answer: What to say when your friendly skeleton leaves on vacation—"BONE VOYAGE"

38. **Jumbles:** ANNOY WHOSE TOFFEE MALTED
    Answer: How that tightwad saved money, even on his honeymoon—HE WENT ALONE

39. **Jumbles:** OLDER MINOR ADDUCE FINALE
    Answer: What's the best dish to get at a "greasy spoon" restaurant?—A CLEAN ONE

40. **Jumbles:** DOUBT FRUIT JETSAM HAGGLE
    Answer: What many "old saws" have done—LOST THEIR TEETH

41. **Jumbles:** LOUSE WEIGH SYSTEM IGUANA
    Answer: Some guys are wise, and some are this—"WISE GUYS"

42. **Jumbles:** SYNOD HAREM SAILOR NEPHEW
    Answer: What an old-fashioned husband expects his wife to do—HELP HIM WITH THE DISHES

43. **Jumbles:** TULIP FAINT METRIC ALIGHT
    Answer: Some people are tactful, while others do this—TELL THE TRUTH

44. **Jumbles:** GLAND YOUNG EXTANT COERCE
    Answer: What happened to those executives when there was a takeover at the food-processing company—THEY GOT "CANNED"

45. **Jumbles:** SIXTY MINER PLOVER DULCET
    Answer: A man usually can't think straight when he only has this—CURVES ON HIS MIND

46. **Jumbles:** FUSSY LAUGH BAUBLE GIMLET
    Answer: He who indulges—BULGES

47. **Jumbles:** HONOR FLOOR DIMITY OUTBID
    Answer: This might be more appreciated if we were given it later in life—YOUTH

184

48. **Jumbles:** CRIME FORCE PRIMED ENTAIL
Answer: He's supposed to be working at the dock for pay, but he prefers to do this—"FREE" LOAD

49. **Jumbles:** DIRTY QUEER VELLUM SEXTON
Answer: Why his conscience was clean— HE NEVER USED IT

50. **Jumbles:** FUZZY HUMAN AVOWAL DROPSY
Answer: What that buffet dinner was sort of— "LAP-HAZARD"

51. **Jumbles:** LIGHT AGLOW GIBBON INTONE
Answer: What some evening dresses are— MORE GONE THAN GOWN

52. **Jumbles:** KNIFE INLET ABACUS GROTTO
Answer: Where the fanatic's train of thought always ran—ON A SINGLE TRACK

53. **Jumbles:** CUBIC WINCE ENTITY AGENDA
Answer: Her promise to be on time carried a lot of this—"WAIT"

54. **Jumbles:** MESSY DOWDY TIDBIT SUNDAE
Answer: What the epidemic of measles in Geneva created—DOTTED SWISS

55. **Jumbles:** BASIN KNOWN CORPSE FACING
Answer: What he was as a result of teaching his teenager to drive—A WRECK

56. **Jumbles:** TRYST TIGER NEARBY TINGLE
Answer: What she served the handsome depositor with—INTEREST

57. **Jumbles:** NAVAL TABOO COHORT DAWNED
Answer: What the snowball fight proved to be— A COLD WAR

58. **Jumbles:** NOOSE NIECE TARTAR FERVOR
Answer: The part of the book the podiatrist liked best— FOOTNOTES

59. **Jumbles:** YODEL EXACT OPAQUE PYTHON
Answer: What do you call an officer who lost the key to his house?—A "COP OUT"

60. **Jumbles:** UPPER TROTH BIGAMY IMPUGN
Answer: What he did when he ran into his pal— PUT THE BITE ON HIM

61. **Jumbles:** HAVEN TEPID GENDER UNHOLY
Answer: Penthouse dwellers usually pay this— HIGH RENT

62. **Jumbles:** EVENT FLOOR FITFUL TANKER
Answer: One of the identical twins was five feet tall— what was the other?—FIVE FEET, TOO

63. **Jumbles:** MAUVE TRULY SCHEME REDEEM
Answer: People in love seldom travel in these— THREES

64. **Jumbles:** SUEDE LILAC ADROIT RARITY
Answer: What some people travel in while remaining at home—TRAILERS

65. **Jumbles:** BYLAW PIOUS GRIMLY SCORCH
Answer: What a crime wave gets in the newspaper— A BIG SPLASH

66. **Jumbles:** ENTRY CATCH MISFIT EXHALE
Answer: High heels can often be this— "ARCH" ENEMIES

67. **Jumbles:** FLANK SWOOP FEUDAL PODIUM
Answer: In the theater these mean no work and no play—FLOPS

68. **Jumbles:** TAWNY PIECE BOUNTY TOWARD
Answer: What the umpire turned pizza chef announced—"BATTER UP!"

69. **Jumbles:** DEITY VITAL RAREFY EXTENT
Answer: His business success depends on driving customers away—A TAXI DRIVER

70. **Jumbles:** VOUCH GLADE TARGET AROUSE
Answer: What the lumberjack went downstream on— A "TRAVELOG"

71. **Jumbles:** TWILL METAL FIASCO HANDLE
Answer: What a deep-sea diver must do when he has a problem—FATHOM IT

72. **Jumbles:** FEWER LYING HUNTER ABOUND
Answer: What do you call a humorist with a split personality?—A HALF WIT

73. **Jumbles:** PENCE UTTER FABLED EFFIGY
Answer: What the new owner of the rundown steak house tried to do—BEEF IT UP

74. **Jumbles:** QUAIL LOGIC CANKER LOCATE
Answer: What the camera club members called themselves—A CLICK CLIQUE

75. **Jumbles:** INEPT LEECH DIGEST CLAUSE
Answer: The flaw in the butcher's golf game— HIS SLICE

76. **Jumbles:** MOUND CHEEK EMBODY BEHAVE
Answer: How the lazy gardener felt about his work— HOE HUM

77. **Jumbles:** OUTDO PATIO INVENT FINERY
Answer: What the commercial fisherman lived on— NET PROFIT

78. **Jumbles:** GRAIN CHAFE OMELET COERCE
Answer: What the melancholy painter made— A LONG FACE

79. **Jumbles:** DOILY BLESS UNIQUE HAZING
Answer: What the matador turned road builder liked most about his work—THE BULLDOZING

80. **Jumbles:** LEAKY PLAIT AGENDA BEHIND
Answer: This can turn a shoe into a slipper— A BANANA PEEL

81. **Jumbles:** TULLE ANNOY POETIC BAKING
Answer: Birds and computer buffs are both comfortable with this—BEING ON LINE

82. **Jumbles:** SNACK MESSY KOWTOW BRAZEN
Answer: What the bored reporter ended up with— A NEWS SNOOZE

83. **Jumbles:** COACH FEVER REALTY NOTIFY
Answer: Trucks create this wherever they go— "HEAVY" TRAFFIC

84. **Jumbles:** CRUSH GAWKY SCHOOL EFFORT
Answer: A good cameraman will do this— FOCUS ON HIS WORK

85. **Jumbles:** ALIVE OAKEN CHARGE COMEDY
Answer: How their first vacation in years made them feel—"REEL" GOOD

86. **Jumbles:** ADMIT MOUND INVEST ELICIT
Answer: Often heard by a phone solicitor in the middle of the message—THE DIAL TONE

87. **Jumbles:** EIGHT CRAFT HELIUM AWEIGH
Answer: Excess calories can turn into this— A WEIGHT LIFTER

88. **Jumbles:** RIVET BAGGY SHREWD NUDISM
Answer: An after-dinner speaker's remarks can become this—HARD TO DIGEST

89. **Jumbles:** THICK GUILD OMELET VENDOR
Answer: What the nurse did to the skittish patient— NEEDLED HIM

90. **Jumbles:** OUTDO HEFTY SUGARY LACKEY
Answer: Air pollution does this—NO EARTHLY GOOD

91. **Jumbles:** HURRY BASSO GROTTO VESTRY
Answer: The kids said the old fashioned record was— GROOVY

92. **Jumbles:** ELITE UNCLE FAIRLY RAREFY
Answer: A white water adventure usually becomes this—A RAFT OF FUN

93. **Jumbles:** FRAME PAYEE GARBLE BEFOUL
Answer: What you might call the diner's threat at the steakhouse—A LEGAL BEEF

94. **Jumbles:** DITTY NOTCH FAMISH DIGEST
Answer: Why she didn't buy the swimsuit— HINDSIGHT

95. **Jumbles:** TWICE WHOOP HANSOM PERSON
    Answer: Why the fortune tellers did not attend the charity dinner—IT WAS NON-PROPHET

96. **Jumbles:** JEWEL COLON TARTAR RADISH
    Answer: What the students considered the geology professor—DOWN TO EARTH

97. **Jumbles:** SNORT BIPED MISUSE SALOON
    Answer: How the gifted ballet student measured her progress—BY LEAPS AND BOUNDS

98. **Jumbles:** ADAGE ABASH ACCORD FIGURE
    Answer: What the busy counterfeiter did—FORGED AHEAD

99. **Jumbles:** TRUTH SCARF ZEALOT PREACH
    Answer: A barber's shaving skills must be this—RAZOR SHARP

100. **Jumbles:** FELON DECRY BROKER SAILOR
     Answer: When Mom returned from a business trip she was—BACK IN THE "FOLD"

101. **Jumbles:** KNIFE LAUGH AUTHOR PAROLE
     Answer: An experienced pilot can end up here—ON A HIGHER PLANE

102. **Jumbles:** CHICK GORGE MADMAN OUTFIT
     Answer: What a beer brewer needs—A HEAD FOR IT

103. **Jumbles:** BLANK REARM BOLERO MARAUD
     Answer: Union talks often become this—LABORED

104. **Jumbles:** SURLY BALKY DELUXE BABIED
     Answer: A couple of glasses of champagne can leave you like this—BUBBLY

105. **Jumbles:** LARVA CLOVE TANGLE IMPEND
     Answer: How do hobos get about?—THEY TRAMP ALONG

106. **Jumbles:** ELDER QUOTA CONVEX BUSHEL
     Answer: A barber who trims his own hair does this—CUTS OVER HEAD

107. **Jumbles:** OPERA BASIC SLOGAN HITHER
     Answer: What the professors turned the island cruise into—A SCHOLAR SHIP

108. **Jumbles:** SYLPH FORAY LIMPID POLISH
     Answer: Why he sold the garbage dump—HE HAD HIS "FILL"

109. **Jumbles:** NUDGE LYRIC SUNDAE MORGUE
     Answer: What the exotic dancer faced every day—THE SAME OLD GRIND

110. **Jumbles:** AUDIT GROIN ANYHOW MAINLY
     Answer: How hubby took it when she bought an expensive mattress—LYING DOWN

111. **Jumbles:** KINKY GIANT BUTANE DEBTOR
     Answer: What the funeral director considered his job—AN UNDERTAKING

112. **Jumbles:** COVEY BURST CORNER SIZZLE
     Answer: A balmy day forecast can be this—A "BREEZE"

113. **Jumbles:** TOOTH PYLON JAUNTY CORPSE
     Answer: How the Georgia fruit picker felt after a day's work—JUST PEACHY

114. **Jumbles:** DOUSE EXCEL OUTING CALLOW
     Answer: You might say the fashion model was this to his work—WELL SUITED

115. **Jumbles:** VITAL EXTOL PENMAN LAXITY
     Answer: What the taxman gave the doctor—AN EXAMINATION

116. **Jumbles:** TRULY TASTY INTONE PEWTER
     Answer: The president of an electric company can be found here—THE SEAT OF "POWER"

117. **Jumbles:** VILLA MOSSY LEEWAY UNHOOK
     Answer: What sour grapes can turn into—WHINES

118. **Jumbles:** BANAL NERVY GROUCH SMOKER
     Answer: A dancer's performance rests on this—HER LEGS

119. **Jumbles:** TRIPE BOUGH POTENT ALIGHT
     Answer: What the king ended up with when he drank too much—A "TIGHT" REIGN

120. **Jumbles:** TEPID BULGY SHAKEN PODIUM
     Answer: They thought the comedian was this—A "STAND UP" GUY

121. **Jumbles:** SORRY FLAKE BUTTON PAYOFF
     Answer: What the unhappy pilot did—TOOK OFF

122. **Jumbles:** ALIAS AHEAD SUBTLY BESIDE
     Answer: Shared by a busy politician and a counterfeiter—BAD BILLS

123. **Jumbles:** ENACT PARCH ASSURE HEIFER
     Answer: Sought by competing taxi drivers—THEIR FARE SHARE

124. **Jumbles:** METAL SLANT MUFFIN BARREL
     Answer: What the organist was to the marriage ceremony—INSTRUMENTAL

125. **Jumbles:** FOYER CHUTE BASKET BEGONE
     Answer: Why the cop didn't join the neighborhood party—THE BEAT GOES ON

126. **Jumbles:** SIXTY TEASE GENDER PARITY
     Answer: Important for a race horse to make during training—GREAT STRIDES

127. **Jumbles:** ARDOR SOAPY MATURE HERESY
     Answer: What the comic indulged in when the town banned liquor—"DRY" HUMOR

128. **Jumbles:** GUESS FABLE ENTAIL AWHILE
     Answer: The movie star avoided the party because she was—BASH-FULL

129. **Jumbles:** JERKY AFOOT FERVOR MYOPIC
     Answer: What the chief's son was—"FIRE" PROOF

130. **Jumbles:** TOKEN CLEFT BURLAP MYRIAD
     Answer: What the visitors heard at the oil well—"CRUDE" TALK

131. **Jumbles:** KNELL JULEP FLABBY HAIRDO
     Answer: Offered by a shady telemarketer—A "PHONE-Y" DEAL

132. **Jumbles:** UTTER MERGE STURDY JOBBER
     Answer: What he considered the waiter's recommendation—A BUM STEER

133. **Jumbles:** COUGH FEINT POLICY DUGOUT
     Answer: A good way to get to the bottom of things—GO TO THE TOP

134. **Jumbles:** PAGAN LINGO SQUIRM FIRING
     Answer: For pitchers, preseason training begins with this—A SPRING FLING

135. **Jumbles:** CRESS CAPON MOBILE EITHER
     Answer: What the programmer found at the bottom of his snack bag—MICRO-CHIPS

136. **Jumbles:** TAWNY WRATH DECODE TAUGHT
     Answer: Mom and her newborn both needed this—A CHANGE

137. **Jumbles:** GRIEF AFIRE PILLAR KINDLY
     Answer: Sought by airline passengers—A "FARE" DEAL

138. **Jumbles:** BARGE CATCH MAYHEM BUNION
     Answer: This will fire up a boxing crowd—A BIG MATCH

139. **Jumbles:** ABHOR STAID HICCUP AROUND
     Answer: What it takes to wear the latest fashion—A RICH HUSBAND

140. **Jumbles:** TARRY DUCHY SECOND ENSIGN
     Answer: Where the crook appeared on the family tree—ON THE SHADY SIDE

141. **Jumbles:** FEWER FUDGE FATHOM WAITER
     Answer: What the bus driver wanted to tell the rude passenger—WHERE TO GET OFF

142. **Jumbles:** YACHT BEFIT FOURTH NEARLY
     Answer: When he hit the jackpot the gambler's wife said he was—HER "BETTOR" HALF

143. **Jumbles:** CYNIC DOUBT EQUITY UNLOCK
Answer: If you suspect your doctor of being a quack, maybe you'd better do this—DUCK OUT

144. **Jumbles:** KNOWN AVAIL TUMULT BANGLE
Answer: Hard to stop when you give up smoking—TALKING ABOUT IT

145. **Jumbles:** BOGUS SWOOP HECKLE BEETLE
Answer: You might say every self-employed person is this—THE BOSS

146. **Jumbles:** TITLE PIECE PONCHO ADROIT
Answer: What the forecaster ended up with during the summer—A HOT TOPIC

147. **Jumbles:** FAUNA LILAC BUBBLE ENTIRE
Answer: A roomful of frisky cubs can be this—"UN-BEAR-ABLE"

148. **Jumbles:** CARGO BRINY MORBID TORRID
Answer: A piece of gym equipment that can cause pain—A BIG MIRROR

149. **Jumbles:** MERCY BISON MAGNUM POISON
Answer: Might be used by a bowler to pay for a diamond brooch—PIN MONEY

150. **Jumbles:** TOXIN RUSTY NINETY OFFSET
Answer: Important for a perfect wedding—THE RITE SITE

151. **Jumbles:** NEWLY FLAME WOEFUL LEVITY
Answer: Why the skydiver proposed in mid-air—HE "FELL" IN LOVE

152. **Jumbles:** BLIMP RAINY LIQUID FORGOT
Answer: The secretary excelled at this—FILING

153. **Jumbles:** SOOTY APART BEHAVE ENJOIN
Answer: Important for ballet students to do—BE ON THEIR TOES

154. **Jumbles:** OBESE TRYST STUDIO JESTER
Answer: What an incompetent pastry chef should receive—HIS JUST DESSERTS

155. **Jumbles:** CHAIR NOOSE CUDDLE TONGUE
Answer: Produced by the squabbling royal couple—"REIGN" CLOUDS

156. **Jumbles:** TWILL WALTZ SICKEN DEFINE
Answer: What she developed when she took up yoga—A NEW TWIST

157. **Jumbles:** FUZZY PRUNE ABRUPT TUXEDO
Answer: What the cowboy liked to do in his spare time—"BEEF" UP

158. **Jumbles:** CHESS TULIP WISDOM PREFIX
Answer: What the condo board faced when the roof leaked—A "COMPLEX" ISSUE

159. **Jumbles:** WHEEL YOUNG FINITE EIGHTY
Answer: What Mom had when she dismissed the stomach-ache on test day—A GUT FEELING

160. **Jumbles:** YODEL ROACH CALICO INHALE
Answer: What the team called the sports psychologist—THE "HEAD" COACH

161. **Jumbles:** NESTLE INTACT HIDING BYWORD RANCOR PLEDGE
Answer: What the bride and groom wanted at their nuptials—WEDDING PRESENCE

162. **Jumbles:** GENIUS TERROR SCURVY FABRIC DIVERT BEHALF
Answer: The butcher got a raise because he was—A CUT ABOVE THE REST

163. **Jumbles:** SYMBOL UNIQUE GADFLY GRASSY TOTTER MOHAIR
Answer: What the retired couple enjoyed when they won the lottery—THEIR "GOLDEN" YEARS

164. **Jumbles:** SNUGLY PYTHON BISECT BEWARE INVOKE FOSSIL
Answer: He bought the farm because he wanted this—A "GROWTH" BUSINESS

165. **Jumbles:** FIZZLE BARROW EASILY BLEACH DAMASK HAGGLE
Answer: What Dad did while the orthodontist figured the cost—"BRACED" HIMSELF

166. **Jumbles:** BEHIND LOCALE WEDGED BECALM BOUGHT SURELY
Answer: Why the tightrope walker got the loan—HER BALANCE WAS GOOD

167. **Jumbles:** SCHEME TAMPER PARLOR BUTTER CATCHY LICHEN
Answer: The kind of talk the cardiac patients had—HEART TO HEART

168. **Jumbles:** BUOYED LEAVEN AROUSE PRIMED MYSTIC SPONGE
Answer: Enjoyed by a gardener—DAYS OF VINE AND ROSES

169. **Jumbles:** MOROSE METRIC BELIEF GULLET KITTEN DEPICT
Answer: What it takes to be an outstanding mailman—LETTER PERFECT

170. **Jumbles:** JOCKEY LADING FAULTY STODGY CHERUB ROBBER
Answer: Why some dieters take pills—FOR GIRTH CONTROL

171. **Jumbles:** FORKED PAYING PENCIL BECAME DULCET KINGLY
Answer: What the insurance salesman issued at bed time—A BLANKET POLICY

172. **Jumbles:** MEMOIR NAUGHT INFECT QUEASY JUNKET TRICKY
Answer: A model and her dog can be this—QUITE FETCHING

173. **Jumbles:** COMMON MIDDAY SINGLE SULTRY EMBARK TANKER
Answer: What they ended up with when they cleaned the 100-year-old jailhouse—THE GRIME OF THE CENTURY

174. **Jumbles:** CLUMSY LAYOFF DAINTY ZIGZAG FIDDLE JOYOUS
Answer: Practical shoes put her here at the formal dance—ON SOLID FOOTING

175. **Jumbles:** MARROW PURIFY ASTRAY BABOON DELUGE DECEIT
Answer: On his day off, "work" can be this to a couch potato—A FOUR-LETTER WORD

176. **Jumbles:** MIDWAY GENTLE INVERT OUTCRY BANANA GOVERN
Answer: What her flower bed became when she won the contest—A VICTORY GARDEN

177. **Jumbles:** AUBURN PLURAL MEASLY GRATIS SAVAGE IODINE
Answer: How the harpist got the lucrative booking—SHE PULLED STRINGS

178. **Jumbles:** BOUNTY KILLER BEFALL BEACON TACKLE SINFUL
Answer: How he felt when he got his laundry bill—TAKEN TO THE CLEANERS

179. **Jumbles:** COLUMN NIMBLE RADIAL TRUISM ABSURD FLEECE
Answer: The professor skipped classes because he was—"ABSENT" MINDED

180. **Jumbles:** COWARD INNING CANDID GOPHER PIGEON CASHEW
Answer: Where you might end up after your kid hits a home run—WINDOW SHOPPING

187

Need More Jumbles®?

Order any of these books through your bookseller or call Triumph Books toll-free at 800-335-5323.

Jumble® Books
More than 175 puzzles each!

Animal Jumble®
$9.95 • ISBN: 1-57243-197-0

Jammin' Jumble®
$9.95 • ISBN: 1-57243-844-4

Jumble® at Work
$9.95 • ISBN: 1-57243-147-4

Jumble® Fever
$9.95 • ISBN: 1-57243-593-3

Jumble® Fiesta
$9.95 • ISBN: 1-57243-626-3

Jumble® Fun
$9.95 • ISBN: 1-57243-379-5

Jumble® Grab Bag
$9.95 • ISBN: 1-57243-273-X

Jumble® Jamboree
$9.95 • ISBN: 1-57243-696-4

Jumble® Jubilee
$9.95 • ISBN: 1-57243-231-4

Jumble® Junction
$9.95 • ISBN: 1-57243-380-9

Jumble® Madness
$9.95 • ISBN: 1-892049-24-4

Jumble® Mania
$9.95 • ISBN: 1-57243-697-2

Jumble® See & Search
$9.95 • ISBN: 1-57243-549-6

Jumble® See & Search 2
$9.95 • ISBN: 1-57243-734-0

Jumble® Surprise
$9.95 • ISBN: 1-57243-320-5

Romance Jumble®
$9.95 • ISBN: 1-57243-146-6

Sports Jumble®
$9.95 • ISBN: 1-57243-113-X

Summer Fun Jumble®
$9.95 • ISBN: 1-57243-114-8

Travel Jumble®
$9.95 • ISBN: 1-57243-198-9

TV Jumble®
$9.95 • ISBN: 1-57243-461-9

Oversize Jumble® Books
More than 500 puzzles each!

Colossal Jumble®
$19.95 • ISBN: 1-57243-490-2

Generous Jumble®
$19.95 • ISBN: 1-57243-385-X

Giant Jumble®
$19.95 • ISBN: 1-57243-349-3

Gigantic Jumble®
$19.95 • ISBN: 1-57243-426-0

Jumbo Jumble®
$19.95 • ISBN: 1-57243-314-0

The Very Best of Jumble® BrainBusters
$19.95 • ISBN: 1-57243-845-2

Jumble® Crosswords™
More than 175 puzzles each!

Jumble® Crosswords™
$9.95 • ISBN: 1-57243-347-7

More Jumble® Crosswords™
$9.95 • ISBN: 1-57243-386-8

Jumble® Crosswords™ Adventure
$9.95 • ISBN: 1-57243-462-7

Jumble® Crosswords™ Challenge
$9.95 • ISBN: 1-57243-423-6

Jumble® Crosswords™ Jackpot
$9.95 • ISBN: 1-57243-615-8

Jumble® Crosswords™ Jamboree
$9.95 • ISBN: 1-57243-787-1

Jumble® BrainBusters™
More than 175 puzzles each!

Jumble® BrainBusters™
$9.95 • ISBN: 1-892049-28-7

Jumble® BrainBusters™ II
$9.95 • ISBN: 1-57243-424-4

Jumble® BrainBusters™ III
$9.95 • ISBN: 1-57243-463-5

Jumble® BrainBusters™ IV
$9.95 • ISBN: 1-57243-489-9

Jumble® BrainBusters™ 5
$9.95 • ISBN: 1-57243-548-8

Hollywood Jumble® BrainBusters™
$9.95 • ISBN: 1-57243-594-1

Jumble® BrainBusters™ Bonanza
$9.95 • ISBN: 1-57243-616-6

Boggle™ BrainBusters™
$9.95 • ISBN: 1-57243-592-5

Boggle™ BrainBusters™ 2
$9.95 • ISBN: 1-57243-788-X

Jumble® BrainBusters™ Junior
$9.95 • ISBN: 1-892049-29-5

Jumble® BrainBusters™ Junior II
$9.95 • ISBN: 1-57243-425-2

Fun in the Sun with Jumble® BrainBusters™
$9.95 • ISBN: 1-57243-733-2